W9-DHX-324

Every Other Man❀

❀ *Half the men in a recent national survey said that they had cheated on their women. Two-thirds said they would cheat under cetain circumstances.*

—FROM "BEYOND THE MALE MYTH:
A NATIONWIDE SURVEY"

Every Other Man

MARY ANN BARTUSIS, M.D.

Thomas Congdon Books E. P. DUTTON New York

The identities of patients mentioned in this book have been disguised to protect their privacy.

For information contact: E. P. Dutton, 2 Park Avenue,
New York, N.Y. 10016

Library of Congress Cataloging in Publication Data

Bartusis, Mary Ann.
Every other man.

"Thomas Congdon books."
1. Adultery—United States. 2. Sex in marriage. I. Title.
HQ806.B37 1978 301.41'53'0973 77-28969

ISBN: 0-525-10064-4
Published simultaneously in Canada by Clarke, Irwin & Company Limited, Toronto and Vancouver
10 9 8 7 6 5 4 3 2 1
FIRST EDITION

TO BART, *my husband,*
whose understanding and patience
have helped us survive this
extramarital affair.

Contents

Acknowledgments

I wish first to thank my patients, those women who came to me for help in coping with unfaithful men. I learned from their experience, and in this book I try to pass along to the reader advice that proved useful to them.

I am indebted to the following people, without whom this book could not have been written:

William Hoffer, who skillfully and agreeably helped me with my manuscript, and to his wife Edie, who often transported it between us and otherwise supported this endeavor.

Jacqueline Simenauer, of Psychiatric Syndication Service, Inc., my literary representative, who prompted me to undertake the book and who brought me to my publisher.

Lillian Rahm, my devoted secretary, who sustained me through those times when my confidence in the book was ebbing and whose comments were of great value.

My four children, who had to listen to endless discussions of the book and for nine months must have wondered if there was anything else going on in the world.

My parents, whose own marriage, with its acceptance and sharing of responsibilities, contributed so fundamentally to my understanding.

Tom Congdon and Deborah Prigoff, whose editorial guidance helped me bring forth the book I wanted to produce.

And the many people at E. P. Dutton who are helping it reach the women I hope it will assist.

Why I Wrote This Book

I have been a practicing psychiatrist for twenty years. Most of my patients are adult women. At least eighty percent of them have experienced the anger, pain, and rejection that women commonly feel when they believe that their men have cheated on them. They come to me to try to put some order into their disrupted lives.

Typically these women are deeply embarrassed. What they seldom realize is that their situation is not unusual or exceptional but that, as victims of cheating, they are probably in the majority. In a recent national survey (*Beyond the Male Myth: What Women Want to Know about Men's Sexuality, A Nationwide Survey,* by Anthony Pietropinto, M.D., and Jacqueline Simenauer,

Times Books), half of the men admitted that they had cheated on their women (one can only guess how many men were unable to admit it) and two-thirds said they would cheat under certain circumstances. If the women in the lives of these men, and in the lives of uncounted other men like them, knew the dimensions of the problem, they might not feel so humiliated.

Indeed, it is perhaps the rare person whose life has not been touched by infidelity, one way or the other. Sociologists predict that by 1980, there will be forty million divorced men and women in America. Many of the divorces are granted openly on grounds of adultery, but infidelity also plays a role in divorces ostensibly obtained because of mental cruelty and incompatibility and even in cases of no fault. And then there are the children of these broken marriages, tens of millions of them. Many of these, too, can be considered casualties of adultery. If one adds to the divorce statistics the many millions of men and women who remain in troubled marriages for financial or religious reasons, for the sake of the children, or merely because the thought of divorce is too devastating, it is easy to see that cheating affects a great number of Americans today. But although adultery is exceedingly common, most people cannot accept it and still have not learned to cope with it.

In another nationwide survey, conducted by Woman-Poll in 1977, more than one thousand women were asked how they would respond to the knowledge that their husbands had cheated. Nine percent said they would ignore the evidence. Ten percent said they would file for divorce. But nearly seventy percent said they would try to find out *why* the affair took place before they would make any judgments about the future of the marriage. This book is written to help women discover why, as well as what to do.

The reader may ask why this book is addressed to women, when many men are victims of adultery, too. The answer is that, judging by what we know, men in our culture seem far more likely to be unfaithful, and in any case, in quantitative terms, women seem to be the ones who are really hurting; so this book is directed to them. But I think that men whose women have been unfaithful could benefit from reading this book; in much of it, the roles are easily reversed, and so much of what is said applies generally to humankind.

It might also be asked why this book so often speaks of *wives* rather than simply of *women*. Women who are not married to the men they love can be just as anguished by male infidelity as a wife can. Yet I have found it impossibly clumsy to try and cover all categories and conditions in one set of terms, and the "classic" affair does involve a husband who is involved with a woman who is not his wife. Much of what is true for wives is true for women in general, and I hope the latter will feel themselves welcomed to these pages.

I want to extend a particular welcome to the woman who doesn't think she needs this book at all—the woman who considers herself happily married and immune to the peril of adultery. To this woman I say: it could happen to you. *Every* woman needs to understand those factors that lead to infidelity, in order to strengthen her relationship and help prevent infidelity from happening to her. *No* woman should take her lover for granted.

I might even suggest that if you are afraid to read this book, it may be a sign that, without consciously knowing it, you are already contributing to the possibility that infidelity will occur.

Let me tell you just a bit about the book itself. Through the years, while helping women with this problem, I have come to recognize a pattern in the emotional responses that seem to follow the disclosure of an affair. I have developed a step-by-step approach to enable women to deal with their reactions—their hurt and anger and feelings of failure, and to learn from the crisis. *Every Other Man* * is based on that course of therapy. For some, the book will be all the outside help needed to resolve the crisis. For others, additional counseling by a trained therapist may be required.

The first chapters, presented mostly in question-and-answer format, deal with the immediate consequences of adultery. They are designed to help answer those painful questions that confront both the man and the women in the tormented days and weeks just after the affair is revealed. The middle of the book will help you find answers to that one burning question: *why?* Three detailed case histories are presented to illustrate how strong, hidden forces often push men and women toward trouble. Without an understanding of these factors, you may find it difficult to make the right decisions about the future. The book's final chapters attempt to guide you to a resolution of the crisis.

As you read, you may feel many of the same emotions that my patients experience. Often during therapy, a patient cancels an appointment for no apparently good reason. Every counselor is familiar with this phenomenon. It usually indicates that the patient is getting close to recognizing some truth that hurts too much to face. This is a critical point in treatment, and you may reach this point as you read. If you find yourself uneasy about some of the material, you may be trying to avoid facing reality. I encourage you to read on with an open mind, even if your journey through the book is difficult and painful. In the end, if you are honest with yourself, you should be better equipped to face this challenge to your happiness.

MARY ANN BARTUSIS, M.D.
December, 1977

PART I

DISCOVERY

CHAPTER 1

Suspicion

I've heard that some men just cannot be faithful, no matter how hard they try. Can I realistically expect my husband to be faithful to me?

It is true that some men seem unable to remain faithful. I believe this is because they suffer from emotional deficiencies. But if a man has a reasonably healthy personality, is attracted to you, loves you, and has committed himself to you, you have a right to expect him to be faithful, just as he expects you to be.

If you are married, your man has vowed to be faithful. If you are engaged, he has promised you his love exclusively. If you are living together without being married, there has probably been an emotional commitment to one another. If the man in your life has been unfaithful, he has betrayed that commitment. You must then determine whether you want the relationship to continue. If he has a basically stable personality, he may merely have made a mistake that the two of you can rectify with a lot of hard work. But if he is the kind of man who "cannot" remain faithful, or if he is no longer in love with you, you will either have to disentangle yourself from the relationship or reconcile yourself to his continued cheating.

My husband is always flirting with other women, even when I'm around. He says it's just innocent fun. Is it an indication that he is cheating?

It may or may not be. There are men who have learned to play this game over many years, and they sometimes find it hard to stop. If you know your husband well enough and remember that he has always flirted, this behavior may be a habit rather than a sign of cheating. On the other hand, if he begins to flirt when he has never done so before, it may indicate an emotional crisis. Your husband possibly views a woman's response to his flirting as reassurance that he is still sexually attractive.

One man I treated saw each woman's response to him as a "goal." He was an aging ex-football player who felt he was still out on the field "scoring." He was embarrassed when he realized this association and stopped his flirting immediately.

How do I know if my husband has been cheating?

There are no absolute answers. The first clues can

be very subtle ones that signify that some sort of change has taken place. Let me illustrate.

We have a poodle named Bijou. Monday through Friday, Bijou watches our morning routine from her favorite position on the floor. My husband, Bart, grabs a second cup of coffee before he leaves for the office. The children wait impatiently for the arrival of the car pool that takes them to school. Bijou lies lazily on the floor, even though the milkman clanks his bottles on the porch and my cleaning lady walks in the back door and my patients begin the daily trek into my office. Not a stir from Bijou.

But on weekends, the routine is different. Bart may work around the house in his jeans. The kids may be at the shore, or, if they are home, they are still asleep. Bijou fidgets nervously. If a patient has to pick up an emergency prescription from my mailbox, Bijou goes wild. Instinctively, she knows things are different. Whatever happens, she wants to be prepared for it.

People are like animals, too. They know when the behavior of those around them is changing. Why does a baby fuss and cry when his parents are rushing around getting ready to go out? He senses change.

A change in behavior patterns is the *single most important* early warning sign that something is happening that may affect your marriage. My patients often say to me: "My husband seems touchy and irritable, and he loses his temper at the drop of a hat!" Or, "He picks at me and the kids—he criticizes us for every little thing we do wrong!" Or they tell me that he just sits by himself and doesn't want to be bothered by his family. He answers questions in one or two words. A good night's sleep, his favorite dinner, tickets to a football game—none of the standard cures for the blues seems to help. All of these complaints are expressions of awareness of change.

Should I accuse him of cheating at this point?

No. There could be a thousand different reasons for his behavior. Chances are that the change is only temporary—that he will work out his problems. But you should remain alert to his actions.

What are some of the signals that a man is cheating?

If a man is involved with another woman, the changes may become more pronounced as time passes. You may overhear him talking quietly into the phone at times, although he usually speaks loudly. He may make a point of picking up the mail himself, although he used to let others in the family do so. He might stay at work later. His business trips may be extended—perhaps he no longer catches the first plane back after the convention. His dinner club meetings might end later and later. Perhaps *Gentlemen's Quarterly* or *Playboy* suddenly appears on his bureau, and he begins to ponder whether a specific tie will go with a certain suit (or he may become sloppier, rather than neater). He may suddenly buy new underwear to replace his old shorts.

His sexual attitudes might become more liberated. He may suddenly attempt radically new techniques in bed. He might say, "Oh, I'm not so sure that this idea of swinging or wife swapping is so bad after all."

You may feel there is no longer any intimate sharing of emotions (if, indeed, there ever was). He may seem to be guarding a secret. There are a thousand and one little hints that can give rise to a feeling of uneasiness and suspicion.

I do suspect my husband of cheating, but I have no real proof. Why do I feel so guilty?

Feeling guilty about your suspicion is quite common, but you shouldn't. Suspicion is the first step toward resolving the hidden problems in your marriage. But you should always give your husband the benefit of the doubt (and vice versa). If your suspicions are raised only once in a while, or if they last only a short time, there is probably a perfectly reasonable explanation that does not involve a lover. Maybe your husband has been secretive because he has planned a surprise birthday party for you. Maybe he has been preoccupied with a major task at the office. Maybe he just heard a lecture on the radio by a female psychiatrist on the subject "Don't Take Your Wife for Granted." His change could be caused by a physical illness or an emotional crisis that may or may not involve a lover.

A certain amount of suspicion can be healthy. It forces you to examine the progress of your marriage. It keeps you on your toes. If you are afraid to face the possibility of adultery in your marriage, then you may have emotional insecurities that could contribute to an affair. You should not be so naive that you deny the evidence of blatant adultery. For only when you face the fact of infidelity can you begin to cope with it. There are things you can do now. They may be painful, but they hurt less than a constant denial of reality.

But is it possible to be *too* suspicious?

Yes. And the danger lies in assuming that your suspicions are correct. If your husband was merely considering an affair, your hostile attitude may actually drive him into the arms of another woman.

A patient I will call Jane came to see me early one January morning. With the aid of a lot of gentle questioning on my part, she managed to tell me her story. She said she first began to suspect her husband Harry of adultery a few weeks before Christmas. First she saw a check for $250 written to "Cash." Harry had not told her about the withdrawal, as he usually did. Then he received a phone call at home one evening from his secretary. He worked late several other nights in a row on a "big contract." He seemed distant and unwilling to talk. He was tired and irascible.

One afternoon Jane happened to drive past an apartment building about a mile from her home and saw Harry's car in the parking lot. She went home shaking with anger. The following Saturday Harry shoveled snow out of the driveway and then announced that he was going Christmas shopping. He was gone six hours and ten minutes, Jane told me. And the next day she noticed that he had two pairs of shorts in the laundry.

Harry said he was staying late at the office on New Year's Eve for a party. But about four o'clock in the afternoon, Jane happened to glance out the window. She saw Harry drive right past the house, his beautiful young secretary snuggled next to him.

The story sounded like a rather ordinary affair between a husband and his secretary. But a psychiatrist quickly learns to take nothing for granted. We all come to conclusions from what we see and hear and then assume those conclusions to be correct. Therefore we pick out the details that prove that we are right, avoiding all other evidence to the contrary.

I tried to help Jane give Harry the benefit of the doubt. Would her story hold up under gentle cross-examination? "That check for $250 . . . couldn't that have been for Christmas shopping?" I asked her.

"Well . . . I guess so. He did give me several expensive pieces of jewelry."

"What about the 'big contract'? Was it real?"

"Oh, yes. Harry closed a deal for $200,000. It was the biggest sale the company has ever made. But that doesn't mean he had to work late all those nights . . . with his secretary."

"But he could have been working?"

"Yes."

"He could have been tired and grumpy from overwork?"

"Y-yes."

"That day you saw his car at the apartment building. Are you sure it was his?"

"It was a blue Cougar." Her voice grew menacing. "I'd know that car anywhere."

"Did you see the license plate?"

"No. But it was his car."

"The day that he had two pairs of shorts in the laundry . . . he was shoveling snow. Was he working so hard that he perspired?"

"Yes." There was uncertainty in her voice now.

"New Year's Eve . . . Did you actually see Harry's face when the car drove by?"

"No." She paused thoughtfully.

I didn't quite know what to believe. It seemed possible that Jane was convicting Harry solely on circumstantial evidence. Was Harry so stupid that he would drive his girl friend right past his home? How could Jane be positive that the man in the fast-moving car was really her husband?

It took many months of weekly sessions with Jane before I managed to find a basis for her fears. It seemed that several years earlier she and Harry had held a New Year's Eve party. At the stroke of midnight, she allowed a neighbor to kiss her. Jane's problems stemmed from the simple fact that she was aroused by his kiss and enjoyed it. She felt guilty—as guilty as if she had gone to bed with him—because she was raised to believe that once a woman was married she should never look at another man, let alone be turned on by him. Jane considered herself despicable for having had a perfectly normal human sexual response. Naturally she thought her husband would lose interest in such an unworthy person.

Jane had struggled with these unreasonable anxieties, and as this particular holiday season approached, she experienced what psychiatrists call an anniversary reaction. Her memories of the painful New Year's Eve experience caused her mind to jumble up the facts. She felt guilty and wanted to punish herself, so she unconsciously reasoned that Harry would have an affair. She chose this form of punishment because a part of her still wondered what it would be like to have sex with another man. This is a psychological process called *projection*—putting someone else in your place and imagining that he or she is doing what you would secretly like to do.

Harry came in to see me for several sessions. He seemed to be an emotionally strong person, and as far as I could tell, he was not having an affair. I couldn't guarantee that he wasn't, but it seemed unlikely. He admitted, however, that Jane's unfounded suspicions had raised questions in his mind about the stability of his marriage. If she had allowed her behavior to continue, she might well have driven Harry away.

It is important for every woman to guard against the dangers of making a false accusation.

Then wouldn't it be better just to keep my fears to myself?

No. I have seen scores of troubled women come to my office and spend the first forty-five minutes gathering their courage to confess their fears. Then suddenly the secret comes out, amid a burst of tears. Most women have tried to keep their doubts to themselves at first, but they have stored up mountains of anger, frustration, shame, and humiliation. Invariably they feel better once they have told me. Only when you have brought your fears to the surface can you begin to deal with them.

Deep down inside you probably aren't so afraid of and concerned about the physical act of adultery. Sure, it hurts to think of your husband with another woman. It hurts very much. Perhaps on a conscious level, that's what hurts most of all. But if you think about it, you may realize that it is his emotional rejection that hurts far more than his physical rejection. If he has lied to you, you may feel that you will never be able to trust him again. The loss of emotional closeness is what really threatens your marriage. If you can recognize that fact, you can confront your husband with your suspicion in a healthy way, by helping him see that you are far more concerned about your relationship with him than about his relationship with someone else.

Things have been so strained between my husband and me lately. If he's having an affair, aren't our problems his fault?

It is so easy to blame him. It is easy to blame the other woman. It is often far more difficult to look to yourself, for you think you are innocent. Yet the truth of the matter is that it takes three corners to make a triangle. You, your husband, and the other woman all have emotional weaknesses that helped bring about the situation. Whether your own contribution was great or small makes no difference, nor should you be interested in keeping score. The important thing is for you to recognize that you have played some role in creating the situation. (I know it seems unfair. But please read on.) When you tell your husband of your suspicion, you can also indicate your willingness to bear some of the responsibility.

The first thing to do is take stock of your marriage. Be honest with yourself and ask yourself questions such as, How much time have you been spending together? Have you been neglecting each other by spending too much time with the children? Have either of you been facing a career crisis? Have you isolated yourself too much in the home? Have there been any changes in your attitude toward your husband? Are you still in love with, and attracted to, one another? How long has it been since you fixed his favorite dinner? Are you both happy with your sex lives?

If you realize that you have both become careless in working at your marriage, then you have a real basis for discussion.

I'm scared to death of opening a discussion with my husband about adultery. How do I go about it without precipitating a crisis?

Choose a time when you can sit down and talk quietly together—when the kids are in bed and when the television is off. The proper kind of statement would be, "Honey, we don't seem to be talking the way we used to. I wonder what has been happening to us."

Now you have accomplished several things. You have openly stated your real concern. Whether there is another woman does not really matter at this point. You have not put your husband on the defensive by declaring him guilty before all the facts are in. You have indicated that you feel there is *some* problem, but you have not said what you think it is. And you have told him that you are willing to share some of the responsibility for what went wrong.

I followed your advice and told my husband I'm concerned about our relationship. If he is cheating, will he admit it to me now?

Possibly. But remember, he may not be cheating. It is very possible that your husband has allowed thoughts of adultery to enter his mind but has not yet acted upon them. Many of us, like Jane, are totally conditioned to believe that once we fall in love, God forbid we should ever have a sexual feeling for another person. Yet that is basic to human nature. We all can have such moments. We are all vulnerable. But many women have denied having this natural feeling for so long that they have difficulty acknowledging it in their husbands. Your husband is a human being. Human beings have sexual thoughts about others that sometimes go well beyond the traditional moral boundaries.

Perhaps he has his eye on another woman. Maybe he has even taken her to lunch but has not yet started an affair. Your careful handling of your suspicions can show him what he is risking. He may suddenly resolve to work harder to strengthen your marriage. Sometimes a brush with adultery can help a husband and wife begin to focus on how they can pay more attention to each other's needs, though I certainly don't prescribe this for an ailing marriage.

Is it true that a man may actually want to be caught?

Yes, in some cases; and a calm early approach might bring the situation into the open. One woman came to me after she found the condoms her husband had stored in the glove compartment of the car. He never used them with her. Even if he did not realize it consciously, the fact that he left the evidence lying around indicated that he probably wanted to get the problem out into the open.

Why would my husband want to get caught cheating?

Despite all the propaganda in movies and on television, some men find adultery to be no fun at all. They quickly realize that the act of sex means little without the emotional commitment they enjoy with their wives. Others find themselves caught up in a round of secret expenses, hurried liaisons, and phony excuses. Some men find a mistress far more demanding than a wife.

Your husband is experiencing a complex set of emotional reactions that he probably does not fully understand. When he first cheated, he may have felt a sense of exhilaration, a new zest for life. He may even find that his sex drive is stronger with you as well as with the other woman. As long as he believes he can keep his two lives separate, this sense of exhilaration may last. But it is merely a buildup to a very big letdown.

If the other woman begins to pressure him, or if he feels he is in danger of being caught, or if he is suffering unbearable guilt pangs, he may become restless, irritable, confused, and depressed. He may find it difficult to sleep. He may increase his eating, smoking, and drinking.

If your husband basically loves you, and he realizes he has made a mistake, he may welcome the opportunity to bring the situation out into the open.

Then why doesn't he just tell me about his affair?

He may need some gentle prodding. It is a deep, dark secret he has been living with. He is scared. You must allow him to confess his affair to you in the manner that is least threatening to him. A conversation about the quality of your marriage gives him that chance. Try to hold back any open accusation of adultery in that first talk. He will understand the implications of your questions, anyway. By restricting your comments to the quality of your marriage, you show him what is most important to you. But if he does not respond, even after you have given him a few days to think things over, you may have to attempt a second, more pointed discussion.

My husband and I aren't used to talking about our marriage. How can I have such a discussion with him?

It may not be easy. In fact, it may be one of the most difficult things you have ever done. If you and your husband have been distant for years, talking seriously now may be almost impossible. But you must try. Remember that your marriage is at stake, so you cannot hold your suspicions inside any longer. Be prepared to state *your* feelings about what is happening to your relationship. For example, you can say, "I've been feeling very uneasy and nervous because we don't seem to be as close as we used to. We aren't spending as much time together, and when we *are* together, I feel that something is coming between us. Something seems missing. I never used to think about our relationship. It just *was*. But now I'm questioning it and beginning to worry about it. I wake up and go to bed with it on my mind. I wonder if you don't feel the same way. Or is it just me?"

I asked my husband what's wrong with our marriage and he didn't respond. What's the next step?

You may have to be more specific. You might say quietly, "I think this change in our relationship may have to do with a number of things. It could be the tension of your job right now. It could be the children. It could be your health. Or it could be that you're having an affair with someone else. Whatever the problem,

I want you to know I'm becoming concerned about it. Honey, is there another woman? Is that the trouble?"

My husband keeps insisting that nothing is wrong between us. What should I do now?

Drop the subject. He can have no doubts about what is bothering you now. If he is having an affair but still denies it, he may need a few days or perhaps a week or so to gather enough courage to tell you and to face the question of what he is going to do about the situation. Let him think about the conversation. Most likely he will soon find a time to talk with you alone. And he will tell you.

How can I possibly work or care for the household during this time?

It will not be easy. But try to maintain your equilibrium. Give him every benefit of the doubt. If you want to save your marriage, you must try harder than ever now. Even if you don't want to save the marriage, the less you disrupt other areas of your life, the better.

What if my husband continues to deny that he is having an affair?

Your husband may be one of those men who will refute your accusations forever, no matter how strong the evidence. Perhaps that is no surprise to you. Maybe you are used to his lying.

The husband of one of my patients, a man I will call Sam, is a typical example. When he was a child, his father told him to lie—or simply not volunteer information—to women, since they could not be trusted with confidential information. His mother cleaned the house, cooked the meals, and changed the diapers, but she never knew how much money was in the checking account. Sam's father never talked to her about business deals, taxes, or car repairs. Naturally Sam grew up believing that his mother didn't have the intellect to grasp the important things in life. When he got married, he never gave his wife Linda the chance to prove otherwise. From the very beginning, Sam kept things to himself, and therefore he found it impossible to trust Linda to cope with the knowledge of his adultery.

A man like this may eventually admit to having an affair if the pressures of his double life grow too great to bear. His telling you is a good sign. It shows that he has broken from the habits of his past and wants to work with you to resolve the problem. But if he still refuses to tell you after you have tried gently but persistently to get the secret out into the open, and if you are 99 percent sure that he is cheating, then perhaps you should discuss the situation with your clergyman, family doctor, or a mental health professional.

Isn't it possible for some men to carry on multiple affairs for years without being caught and without suffering from fear or guilt?

Some men do carry on affairs successfully for years. Often, however, that is because their wives choose to ignore the evidence. Still, it is possible for a man to cheat over a long period of time and get away with it. But I believe that no matter how "successful" he is in his extramarital affairs, he will still experience some difficulties.

For example, a man named Chet came to me for a few

sessions, hoping that I could help him solve his problem. He was married to one woman and having affairs with two others. His problem was that he wanted my advice, as a woman, on how to juggle the three of them simultaneously. What had first seemed like a lark had turned into a nightmare for him. All three women placed demands upon his time and money. One of his lovers kept trying to call him surreptitiously at home. The other kept applying the when-are-you-going-to-divorce-your-wife-and-marry-me pressure. His wife wanted him to spend more time at home with her and the children. To support his expensive habits, Chet had to take a second job that gave him even less time to split among the women in his life. Then he lost a promotion at his main job because his performance had dropped.

When Chet came to me he was drinking heavily, losing sleep, and seemed close to a breakdown. I suggested that he needed help in making a choice among the three women. He decided to shop around for a counselor who would tell him what he wanted to hear—how to find a way to keep all three women. I never saw him again.

Chet was a chronic adulterer. But even the man who truly loves his mistress will rarely remain happy trying to juggle two women. Perhaps he has fallen out of love with his wife yet feels an obligation to remain at home to help raise his children. Or perhaps he genuinely feels he is in love with both his wife and his mistress. But he cannot remain free from guilt and anxiety as long as he tries to live with a secret.

I am absolutely certain that my husband has cheated. Can my marriage be saved?

.re is hope for almost any marriage. But this ques- . cannot be answered easily.

In general, if the affair was an isolated one in an otherwise happy marriage, the outlook is good. But if there has been a continual history of many affairs with many different women, the outlook is poor. No one, however, can look into a crystal ball and tell you the future.

The institution of marriage is currently under severe attack. Divorce statistics explode with more force each year. A large percentage of loving couples now decide to live together rather than to formalize their unions. Can your marriage survive the pressures of modern life? Is it worth saving? Now is the time to take an objective look. The fact that you find yourself in one corner of a triangle does not necessarily mean that your marriage is dying. To be sure, it is critically ill. When a person suffers a heart attack, his chances for survival often depend upon his basic physical strength. When a marriage is ill, its chances for survival depend upon how well both husband and wife have grown together, joining their lives in a strong bond.

There are many other factors you must consider before you can make a knowledgeable decision about the future. Try not to act too quickly. Think. Question. Talk. Try to find out *why*. Later in this book, I will give specific advice to help guide you in determining whether or not your marriage is worth saving.

CHAPTER

2

The Immediate Effects

My husband has admitted his affair. What happens now?

You now begin the long, agonizing process of deciding the future of your marriage. You and your husband may be able to learn from your problems and rebuild the marriage. Or you may call it quits. Regardless of the final outcome, however, the immediate effects will be painful. Adultery is a family affair. It will disrupt the lives of every member of the household. Everyone will suffer emotional side effects during this decision-making period.

I'm so mad at my husband I can't even talk to him. How can we possibly work out a solution?

Anger is usually the first emotion a woman feels when she learns that her husband has been unfaithful. You are human. You need the love and affection of another human being. From your earliest moments, society has probably impressed upon you that your value in life is derived largely (or completely) from your relationship to a man. I do not subscribe to that theory; nevertheless, it is the message of our culture. No woman who has grown up in our society can escape the feeling of anger that comes when she is rejected by *her* man.

Direct expression of that anger is necessary to clear the air. Otherwise you will take it out on the children, the neighbors; your relatives, co-workers, boss; the saleslady, telephone operator; or any casual acquaintance. Unless you let your husband know how you feel immediately, your anger will build and broaden the distance between you.

How should I express my anger?

Say what comes to your mind. For example, "How could you do this to me and the children, after all we've been through together? You're just like your father. He played around for years. I refuse to be treated like this! How could you?" You might shout at the top of your lungs. Your husband probably will not be surprised at such a tirade. He expects it. Naturally, when you are angry, you will have a tendency to hit below the belt. But once you've screamed out all the things that come to mind, you'll have a better chance to sit down and calmly discuss the problem once more.

But what if my husband yells back at me?

You should anticipate that he will, because he needs to find a release from the tension that he has been under. He also needs to defend himself, to look for justification for his infidelity.

Will my anger prevent us from working out a solution?

It may. For a time, your anger may keep you from making any progress toward resolving the crisis. But if you vent your anger directly, and allow your husband to do so also, it should subside over a period of several days or weeks. Your husband feels very guilty right now, and he knows your anger is justified.

On the other hand, if you make him feel that you will punish him for the rest of his life or that you will use his affair as an excuse to pour out all your other frustrations on him, he may decide to leave you.

What do you mean by my "other frustrations"?

You may, for example, already be worried about your sick mother or not getting a promotion at work, or be having trouble with a neighbor or arguing with your oldest daughter. The frustration and anger from these other situations can build up and be taken out on some other person if he or she hasn't been dealt with directly. Those feelings may cause you to show more anger toward your husband over his affair than is really warranted.

What can I do about my pain?

It doesn't matter how many books you read or how many people you counsel with—no one can bear the pain for you. Just as you must do with your anger, you must get your pain out into the open. I know of no greater therapy than a good cry. That is generally how a woman spends her first session with me. When you dry your tears, it somehow seems to clear your head, too.

Instead of moping around with the pain, try to do something productive. Find a job that doesn't require your complete concentration—clean out the attic or the garage, rearrange file cabinets at the office, or wash the car. When you are finished, you will at least have the satisfaction of knowing that the hurt didn't get the best of you. As an adult, you should know by now that you can never rid your life of all pain. Learning to tolerate it is half the battle. You may even find that pain is not a wholly destructive phenomenon. Through it, you may begin to see things more clearly and become more aware of yourself as an individual.

But my pain is more physical than emotional. Why does my stomach hurt?

Many of us have learned to bottle up our feelings inside. Often the tension caused by deep emotion causes us physical pain, which we find easier to recognize and understand than emotional hurt. This physical pain is known as psychosomatic disorder.

When you experience bodily pain, you should see a doctor. But if the doctor finds no physical cause, you must accept the possibility that your symptoms are psychosomatic. (Common psychosomatic illnesses are migraine headaches, ulcers, colitis, shortness of breath, and chest pains.) These symptoms create *real* pains. You must not be ashamed of the fact that they may be linked to mental conflict. You should discuss your problems with your doctor, since they may be important clues that will enable him or her to make a diagnosis.

I feel like such a failure. Where did I go wrong?

The average American wife is far too dependent upon her husband. That is why adultery has such a devastating effect upon most wives. The more dependent a woman has been upon her husband, the more she will perceive the death of the relationship as meaning her own death as well. She cannot see herself surviving without her husband. What about money, food, the children? Rejection is very painful even for the emotionally strong woman, but when that woman has built her life totally around one man, his rejection can be, and sometimes is, fatal.

No adult should be that dependent upon someone else. Career women seem to have a somewhat easier time coping with a cheating man. To be totally happy, such a woman may need to depend upon the knowledge that her husband loves her, but she doesn't need him to take her by the hand and lead her through life. She can function quite well by herself. She is able to make her own decisions, have her own ideas, express her own opinions. If something happens to cause the marriage to die, she knows she will still survive. So can you.

Right now, however, try hard to remember that time has a way of healing even the deepest wounds. These are difficult days for you. But time will pass, and so will much of the anger and pain. No matter what happens today, the sun will rise tomorrow. There is a future for you.

I used to feel that I was attractive to my husband. Why do I feel so ugly now?

Our society has created certain artificial standards of physical appearance. A constant flood of propaganda tells us the importance of youthfulness, beauty, and slimness. We are all susceptible to that brainwashing. But the woman who has placed an undue emphasis on her looks is going to have a more difficult time coping with feelings of failure.

One of my patients lost her husband because of such feelings. He had a brief affair, which he had confessed to her. Both husband and wife were coming to see me in an effort to work out their problems. When Laura entered her fifties, a pound or two of flesh appeared where she had not meant it to be. She became very conscious of what she called rolls of fat around her waist, but to me she did not seem overweight at all. Because she was repulsed by her own figure, she assumed that Tom would be. So whenever Tom reached for her, Laura recoiled. Tom decided that Laura no longer loved him because she didn't want to be touched, and he stopped trying to touch her. That, in turn, convinced Laura that Tom no longer loved her. Finally Tom moved out of the house—yet I believe they did still love each other.

I believe that everyone should try to appear as attractive as he or she can without becoming fanatical about it. A good appearance is important, but you must always remember that you had other qualities, too, that attracted your husband in the first place. These are the hidden strengths of your marriage. As your husband's wife, you have shared with him thousands of experiences that form a real basis for love. The memories of courtship, early job experiences, vacations, the birth and care of children, good times at parties, weekends at the beach, and comfortable evenings together at home can build strong bonds between husband and wife. You have what a basketball player would call the home-court advantage.

Perhaps your husband has become infatuated with a more attractive, glamorous woman. Once the early infatuation has cooled—as it usually does—your marriage may prove to be a far stronger attraction.

I'd like to move into a separate bedroom until we resolve this mess. But is that wise—am I driving my husband to seek sex elsewhere?

If you feel you cannot sleep close to him, it would be better to move to the other side of the same bed. Moving out to another room is a type of separation. It could force a premature breakup.

I discovered that my husband made love to the other woman in our bed, when I was visiting a relative. Now I don't want to sleep there. I can't stop picturing the two of them where I'm lying. What should I do?

Buy a new bed. Put it in a different bedroom.

Should I have an affair of my own?

It is a natural, understandable impulse to find a

lover in order to retaliate against your husband. But self-control is necessary, despite your strong feelings. Acting on these feelings will be a symptom of your own emotional instability.

That's not fair, is it?

Of course not. But what is fair in life? If you have an affair of your own, you will compound the problem within your marriage immensely. In addition to all the guilt he may now feel, your husband will experience the same reactions you are having to his adultery. You, in addition to all your anger, fear, and pain, will pile up your own tremendous mountain of guilt. As a result, the marriage will be much harder to save.

Even if your marriage is breaking up, there is a very selfish reason not to run out and have a vindictive affair. Whatever weaknesses there may be in your husband's personality, remember this—you chose him. Until you have learned much more about the causes of your marital problems, until you understand your husband and yourself much better, you may face the danger of choosing another man who has the very same weaknesses as your present husband.

I have seen this happen time and time again. One of my patients was married to a man who would frequently get drunk and beat her and the children. Gail cried out her pain to me in the office, but she only came to see me for a few sessions. Having filed for divorce, she felt ready to begin life anew. But she didn't take the time to search her own personality to discover why she had chosen such a vicious husband in the first place. Before long, she was married a second time, and soon after the wedding, she was back in my office complaining about the same old problem: Her new husband was a wife beater, too.

Before you entangle your emotions with another lover, you must be sure you know what went wrong between you and your present lover.

But I want to be loved. How long must I wait?

What's the hurry? Your marriage may be breaking up—you must face that possibility. But there is also the chance that it will stay together. There is a better chance of a happy ending to this crisis if you control your own natural desire to hurt the man who hurt you. Whatever the outcome, this is not the time to burden yourself with even more emotional pressure.

My husband had hardly finished telling me about what he's been doing before he wanted to make love to me. I find that very insensitive of him. All I can think about is that other woman in his arms and what they do together. Am I wrong to deny him?

He may not be insensitive. He may be one of those individuals who uses sex as an escape from an unpleasant situation. Or he may see this as a way of making up, of saying, "I'm sorry." In any case, you are not wrong to deny him if sex will make you very uncomfortable. But you should let him know that the feelings you have at the moment may change. Say something like, "The way I feel, I just can't go to bed with you now." The word *now* implies that your rejection of his advances may be only temporary.

Should I try to watch my husband more closely now that he has cheated?

This is a difficult question. Because your suspicions have been justified, it will be natural for you to want to keep tabs on your husband. But such behavior can be counterproductive. The more pressure you apply, the more he may want to escape from the marriage. In addition, if a man really wants to cheat, he will find a way. You cannot watch him every moment of every day.

Some husbands will go out of their way to let you watch them. One of my male patients had admitted to his wife that he had a brief affair. In the aftermath, he found himself burdened with guilt. He had been raised a strict Catholic, and his affair made him feel so guilty that he could no longer relax around his wife. He went overboard. He began to plague his wife with the precise details of his day at the office. He assured her that he would be home at 5:25. If he went to the store in the evening, he told her exactly where he went, what he bought, and why. Around the house, he jumped at her every word. Though she had not been a suspicious wife in the past, his behavior made her so now.

What should I tell the children about their father's affair?

If you are merely suspicious, I do not believe it is advisable to confide your fears to your children. But once the affair is out in the open, the children's feelings must be considered. They know that something is wrong. Often a child's mind may build the situation into a crisis well out of proportion. Since the children are almost totally dependent upon the two of you for survival, their feelings of abandonment can cause severe problems. So can your efforts to hide your husband's adultery.

You cannot keep reality away from children forever. That is the same as trying to keep them away from funerals. A child should learn about death early, so that he or she will be better able to understand the death of someone close. Similarly, a child should be prepared for the possible death of the marriage.

It sounds very difficult. How can I tell them?

Pick a quiet time in the evening, after dinner. Tell the children that you and their father have something to talk to them about. (If he refuses to cooperate, you will have to handle the task by yourself.) First, ask the children if they have noticed anything different lately. If they have, ask them what they have noticed. Often their responses will help you determine how to begin the discussion.

Trying as much as possible to talk in their own language, you should explain that something is wrong between you and their father; as a result, he thinks—at least sometimes—that he wants to be with another woman. Then say that, naturally, this has been causing a lot of trouble between the two of you. Explain the current status of the situation to them. If the affair is continuing, tell them so. If it is over, tell them that, too. Then explain to them that you are trying to work out the problem together (if, indeed, you are).

You should go on to say that some marriages can overcome such a problem and continue to be happy, but some cannot. It is not too early to prepare them for the possibility of divorce. Many children today have friends whose parents are divorced. They see marriages breaking up all around them, and they need to discuss the possibility of this happening to their family. Answer all their questions as honestly as you can.

How will I know how much to tell my children?

Their questions will provide the clues. These questions will be based upon their age and degree of exposure to the rest of the world. Today, even in the poorest of homes, television has taught children about life. By the time they are four or five years old, they have heard the terms *divorce, prostitute, lover,* and many others. They have witnessed the agony of a custody fight on the afternoon soap operas.

Listen carefully to your children's questions and gear your answers directly to their concerns. For example, a four-year-old might ask, "Does this mean I will have to take my bike back and forth between two houses?" You can assure the child that you and Daddy will work out that problem for him.

An eight-year-old boy might wonder whether Daddy will still go with him to Cub Scout camp. Daddy should (or in his absence you should) reassure the boy that he will try to do what he has already promised.

A thirteen-year-old girl might ask, "Will I have to go visit Daddy on weekends even if I want to stay at my girl friend's house?" Reassure her that you will try to let her make the choice.

A sophisticated sixteen-year-old might simply say,

"It's about time the two of you are finally doing something about your troubles."

Above all, tell the children that both of you still love them and will continue to do so. They must understand that even if the marriage changes, your love for them will not.

My husband refuses to talk to the children with me. What should I do?

You are on your own. Explain to the children that this experience may be so painful and embarrassing for Daddy that he just couldn't face telling them. Tell them you know they will understand that it doesn't mean he no longer loves them.

Won't the children tell all this to their friends?

You can explain to them that some things are family matters and are only to be discussed in detail within the family. If they have more questions later, you will be happy to answer them.

You can be reasonably sure, however, that they will discuss this with at least one best friend. And there is the chance that the story of your marital problems will quickly make its way around the neighborhood (it may already have done so, anyway). Even if they tell, isn't the understanding of your children more important to you than the gossip of your neighbors?

What is going to happen to my family emotionally as a result of this trouble?

A family has a life of its own. It is the sum of the

lives of its members. When the family is threatened, the family members all have a premonition of death. They tend to experience the same feelings of grief they would have if a loved one died. There will be times when you will be too upset to cook dinner. Maybe your husband will be unable to work for a day or two. The children will be moody and perhaps have problems in school. Difficulties like these are to be expected. But as time passes, the trauma should lessen. Our emotions heal just like our bodies. If someone does not experience this natural healing process, he or she may be emotionally ill. There are symptoms you must be alert for. If you see them in yourself or another member of the family, they may indicate that the marital crisis has triggered a pathological depression. Remember, all of us are susceptible to short periods of weakness. But if emotional problems seem to persist, the victims need help.

How can you tell when someone needs help?

Depression, one of the most common reactions to stress, can be signaled by a variety of symptoms, including:

A general and all-encompassing feeling of hopelessness and despair. Life does not seem worth living. There is no way out. It seems as if nothing will make the situation better.

Inability to concentrate. This may show up in attempts to read, write, or converse. An adult may be unable to perform his or her job; children may fail in school.

A change in physical activities. Some people eat more

when they have the blues, others eat less. Some sleep long hours, others have insomnia. Some feel an increased need for sex, others have no interest. Whatever a person's characteristic responses to normal low periods, depression tends to magnify them.

Loss of self-esteem. People may momentarily question their value as human beings, but if they begin to dwell on the belief that they are just not good for anything, they have a problem. In women, this often stems from a tendency to view the relationship with their husbands as the only important thing in their lives.

Withdrawal. I have seen many patients who exhibit a groundless fear that others will reject them, just as their husbands did. So they simply avoid contact with others. Often women stay at home, isolating themselves inside the house. Even at work or school, people can isolate themselves by refusing to pay attention to conversations. But many others, once their suspicions of adultery have been confirmed, will now confide their problems to a good, strong friend whom they can trust. If you have such a friend and are unable to talk about the crisis, it may be a sign of depression.

Oversensitivity. People convince themselves that the whole world is against them. Anything that anyone says or does is interpreted as a hostile act.

Misdirected anger. This is a consequence of oversensitivity. A mother may find herself reacting unreasonably toward her children, friends, or co-workers. It is her husband she is angry with, yet she forces others to suffer instead. Child abuse can be a common consequence of this symptom.

Guilt. When one member of the family begins to feel

totally responsible for the marital crisis, he or she is responding in an unhealthy manner. You must all strike a balance with your emotions. Your husband is not totally guilty, but neither are you. And your children must not be allowed to feel that they are the real cause of the trouble.

Extreme dependence upon others. Helplessness sets in. The victims allow others to care for their needs more and more. They are regressing to childhood.

Threats of suicide. It is very normal to want to be relieved of stress, to go to sleep at night hoping that you don't wake up the next morning. But when that feeling goes one step beyond, there is a problem. When you allow yourself to dwell on thoughts of suicide, or when you make even idle threats of suicide in an attempt to gain your husband's sympathy, you need help.

What other symptoms of depression should I look for?

Other danger signs are extreme nervousness, complaints of aches and pains for which no physical cause can be found, nightmares, fear of going out or being alone, and fear of driving a car. Look for any developing patterns of behavior that are out of tune with your basic personality (or with the personality of others in your family), such as lying when you have previously been the champion of honesty, cheating when you never would have allowed yourself to look at another man, becoming sloppy about your appearance and your home when you have always been a meticulous person. These are further signs of a person's weakening emotional condition. The extreme cases would include people who completely lose touch with reality.

What do I do if I notice any of these signs?

If you feel that you or any other member of your family exhibits prolonged symptoms of a pathological depression, you must seek professional help immediately. Later in this book, we will talk about whether you can benefit from such help. There are many reasons less dangerous than depression to go for counseling. But during the time you are beginning to analyze your marriage and attempting to resolve the crisis, you must be alert for these danger signals in yourself and your family. They can be fatal.

CHAPTER

3

❁

❁*The Other Woman*

I think about the other woman all the time. What's the most sensible attitude toward her?

I find that my patients generally have one of two attitudes concerning the other woman. Some injured wives want to know nothing about her. They order their husbands never to mention her name. Other wives want to know everything, sometimes even the sexual details. They become obsessed with learning what the other woman looks like, and they may even try to arrange a face-to-face meeting. It is not uncommon for a wife to try to kill the other woman, and vice versa. Somewhere amid this range of reactions, you need to develop a healthy response to the threat the other woman poses.

The most important point to remember is that no matter how much you may hate her, she is a human being, too. As far as she is concerned, *you* are the other woman. She may hate you as much as you hate her. She may want to win your husband's love just as much as you do. She may be curious about you, just as you are curious about her. Like you, she has a particular set of emotional strengths and weaknesses. Like you, the entire background of her life set the stage for her present actions.

And, like you, this woman faces a variety of problems as a result of your husband's cheating. She is caught in a web of secrecy that breeds feelings of guilt and anxiety. She must be satisfied with only brief moments of your husband's time—he has probably had to make many last-minute changes in his plans to meet her. She cannot telephone him at home to talk over her personal problems. She cannot run out to dinner with him on the spur of the moment. She has to worry about pregnancy and abortion. She has to worry about the humiliation of being branded as an adulteress in divorce court. And she cannot count on your husband's emotional support to help her make it through most of the lonely nights.

I'm so curious about the woman's appearance. Should I ask my husband to show me a picture of her?

Perhaps you can ask him for a general description. Listen carefully, for I have observed that the other woman's appearance can provide you with an important clue to the future of your marriage. If the other woman is very different from you in her looks—if she is much younger and too obviously sexual—your marriage may stand a good chance of survival. It is likely that he is just seeking fresh sexual stimulation, possibly because some crisis in his life has temporarily upset his normal sex life. He may be having trouble on the job. He may be worried about aging or he may be in a financial bind. Any of these things may have interfered with his sexual performance. Whatever the specific reason, he gave in to the flood of propaganda that tells him his real worth, which he isn't sure about, can be measured by his sexual performance. To bolster his opinion of himself, he had an affair.

But if I'm willing and able to do whatever he wants sexually, why did he turn to the other woman instead of giving me the chance to help him perform better?

First of all, you cannot be sure that his sexual performance has been good with the other woman. Second, he may be suffering from something called the Madonna-harlot syndrome. When a man's self-esteem is low, he may feel that he does not deserve a "good" woman, like you. Only when he is with a "bad" woman, whom he cannot respect, will he be relaxed enough to perform well sexually. It has been my experience that such men will often see the folly of their behavior as their self-esteem improves. Then they will do their best to patch up their ailing marriages.

What else can I learn from the kind of person the other woman is?

Your husband's report on the qualities of the other woman may not be reliable. He may make her seem too good (or he may play down her attributes). But it can be instructive to try to perceive what *he* thinks is so wonderful about her (whether or not you agree). If he thinks she is cultured and intelligent, that may indicate a desire for qualities in his partner that you, so far, to his way of thinking, may not have been able to offer. Sudden changes would be silly and probably futile, but it might be that, in due course, you would decide to pick up this signal from him and develop your tastes and capabilities in various ways.

What if the other woman is similar to me in appearance and background?

Your husband may be turning toward this woman because of his memories of how things used to be between you. He may be trying to recapture lost laughter and mutual interests you used to share. If this is the case, you must ask yourself what happened to the good times. Who or what came between you? Why did he go out looking for a memory of lost love?

My husband is convinced that his new life with the other woman is what he wants. What do I do?

That possibility always exists no matter how hard you might try to save the marriage. If a period of time has passed and he still feels this way, then you must learn to accept it and go on with your own life. But read on, please, before you face that possibility.

I've lost my looks. I know that. My husband had an affair with his secretary, who is a beautiful young woman. How can I hope to compete with her?

You can't, physically. Her outward beauty and youth will win for her in that department. If you expect to keep your husband on the basis of looks alone, your marriage may be doomed. As I said before, I believe you should have a healthy respect for your appearance. If you keep yourself looking the very best you can *for your age,* you will command the respect of everyone—including your husband and yourself. But if you try to compete with a younger woman, you may only succeed in looking ridiculous (such as a grandmother in a mini-skirt).

Remember that the young woman will get old, too. The hope for your marriage lies beyond the realm of beauty. The recent survey on male sexuality, cited in the introduction to this book, found that the majority of American men put a greater value on the concern a wife has for her husband than on how beautiful she is. Your husband needs to feel the value of the love that grew as he shared with you the growth of each new wrinkle and gray hair.

I find that I want to know every detail about my husband's lovemaking with the other woman. It somehow makes it less frightening and brings it down to size. But he begs me not to grill him. Don't I have a right to know everything?

When an injured wife is determined to find out all the details, it is an indication that she is trying to measure herself against the other woman. If you find yourself obsessed with a need to know, perhaps you should look instead at the quality of your own sexual response. Your husband may have felt that you wouldn't try (or enjoy) a certain sexual practice. Rather than share the details of his other sexual experience, maybe you could share his sexual curiosity. Find out what he wants to try, and try it. Your marriage is worth that chance.

My husband admitted to me that he has been with a prostitute. How can I compete with a "professional"?

In some ways, you are lucky. The prostitute is the woman who should cause you the least concern. To her, pleasing your husband—or anybody else—is her job. She provides a service to meet a consumer demand. The successful prostitute usually can compartmentalize her life so that her career does not interfere with her personal life, which could even include her own love affair and marriage. Her prime motivation is money. She feels neutral about most of her clients and usually fakes an orgasm with them. If your husband has patronized a prostitute, you can be reasonably sure she has no intention of stealing him away from you. The business nature of this transaction indicates that your husband desired no emotional experience along with his outside sex.

Why does a married man turn to a prostitute?

There are many reasons. Perhaps he needs the excitement of a new sexual experience because his own wife is unwilling to be adventuresome. Or he may feel the need to enjoy a selfish sexual relationship. Or to escape from the realities of family responsibilities. Or to act out sexual fantasies that he cannot picture his wife accepting. Or maybe he just requires an ego boost.

Or he might be suffering from the Madonna-harlot syndrome. When a man is denied sex because of such occurrences as his wife's illness, a business trip, or military service, he will sometimes turn to a prostitute because he knows there is no danger of becoming involved.

My husband had a one-night stand while he was in another city on a business trip. He met the girl in a bar. How serious a threat is this to our marriage?

If it happened only once, the chances for your marriage to recover are good. The pickup may be a promiscuous woman who needs to be constantly reassured of her desirability or who is searching for an orgasm she never had. She may use sex the way an alcoholic uses liquor. If your husband had a brief fling with a pickup, it was probably quite similar to a prostitute-client relationship.

On the other hand, if this happens frequently, it may indicate that he is on a constant search to prove his own virility with a variety of partners. He probably doesn't really understand himself very well, in which case he needs professional counseling.

What about the man who has carried on a long-standing affair with one woman? Is this more of a threat?

Indeed it is. The mistress may prove to be the most difficult rival. Your husband's continuing affair with her is going to rob you and the children of his affection, time, and money. She may constantly interfere as you and your husband attempt to solve your marital problems. She and your husband are emotionally involved with each other. She may actually be in love with him, perhaps for the very same reasons you fell in love with and married him.

Some mistresses are content to remain in the role of the other woman. When a woman has been raised with a poor image of marriage, she may find herself unwilling or unable to make a long-standing commitment later in life. But many women do want marriage and they see the role of mistress only as a temporary means of winning your husband away from you. Try to remember that there are psychological roots to the mistress's behavior, just as there are to yours and your husband's. This may keep you from becoming the stereotypically bitter, resentful wife.

What if the other woman is my best friend?

Obviously, she won't remain so. If the affair is out in the open, then all three of you should discuss it and come to some agreement about the future. If she doesn't know that you have discovered the affair, then your husband has an obligation to tell her. If he refuses, you can go directly to her and discuss the situation. You must find out what her plans are. Is she intent on winning your husband away from you? Has she been satisfied as his mistress? Is the affair continuing, or is it over? These are questions that must be answered before you can proceed.

What if he is involved with his ex-wife?

This is a difficult problem. It means that your husband probably never settled in his mind the conflicts that caused his divorce. Or it may indicate that he is guilt-ridden and cannot let go. This may prove to be a very unyielding triangle, and getting professional help is the logical step to take.

My husband wants to see the other woman. Should I forbid him to see her?

No. Forbidden fruits always appear to be sweeter. If you give him an ultimatum, you may push him right into her arms. If he insists on continuing the affair, you may want a separation. Fine. You can talk with him about *your* relationship. But let him make the decisions about *their* relationship.

My husband gave his girl friend several gifts. Should I make him ask her to return the things he has given her?

I recommend that you don't. It may be true that he spent money on her that he should have spent on his own family. But I believe it is better just to forget about those things and try to patch up your marriage.

One of my cases provides a good example. George had a rather long affair with a woman at his office. But he made up his mind to give up the affair and work to strengthen his relationship with his wife, Helen. Helen was understandably bitter, and she wanted to strike back at the other woman. During the affair, George had allowed his mistress to borrow his boat, which was harbored on the Delaware River. As a means of assuring herself that the affair was over, Helen demanded that George force the woman to return the extra key to the boat. She nagged at George to get the key back because the boat took on a symbolic meaning for her. As long as the other woman had a copy of the key, Helen felt threatened. But her constant nagging was not the sort of support that George needed in his efforts to break off the affair. Worse, Helen was forcing George to see the woman again! I tried to get Helen to forget about the key, at least for the time being, but she kept pressuring George until finally, in disgust, he moved out of his house and into his mistress's apartment.

Helen didn't only lose the boat. She lost George too.

I desperately want to phone the other woman and tell her just what I think of her. Any reason why not?

Yes. By creating a scene, you will only lower your husband's respect for you. And it won't do any good, either. The other woman might say, "No wonder he can't live with his wife anymore."

It would be better for you to scream out your hatred alone in your room, or perhaps work it off with hard physical labor.

What should I do if the other woman calls me?

Do your best to maintain your dignity. The first time she calls, don't hang up on her. And don't blast her with a barrage of choice names. Let her talk awhile. Take this opportunity to listen closely to what she is saying and how she is saying it. Don't ask questions about her and your husband, for she will only embellish the details. After you have listened politely for a few minutes, simply say courteously, "I'm sure my husband and I will be able to work something out," or, "This is something for my husband and me to handle." Then get off the phone, have a good cry, and congratulate yourself for not losing your cool.

If she persists in calling, tell her that you do not appreciate harassment and hang up. If this continues, you may have to refuse to answer the phone when you think it might be her calling.

No matter how I try, I just cannot bring myself to go into a room, restaurant, store, or church where she has been or where she might show up. What should I do about this feeling?

It would be easy if I could simply tell you to avoid those places. If it is only *one* store or *one* restaurant, then don't go there. But if your repulsion gets carried away and you won't even travel down the same highway because you may see her, then you have more serious symptoms that may require professional help.

My husband says that his mistress has threatened to kill herself if he doesn't come back to her. How should I handle this?

When the other woman fears that she is losing out, she may resort to this ploy. She may well see it as a means of winning back your husband's attention.

There is little you can do in this situation except empathize with your husband. You must let him decide how to respond. Whether her threat is real or imaginary, if you stand in your husband's way, you will appear to be vicious and cruel. But if you allow him to deal with the threat, and if you can even bring yourself to let him discuss it with you, you will gain respect in his eyes. It isn't going to be easy to step aside at this point, but it is very necessary.

An "other woman" came to my office one day seeking a prescription for sleeping pills. I do not dispense them freely. I asked her to sit down and tell me why. She sobbed out her story. She was a secretary. For more than a year, she had been having an affair with her boss. She knew that he was unhappy with his marriage, and she had figured that he would divorce his wife and marry her. Now he had called off the affair and warned that he would fire her if she caused any trouble.

"Why do you need the pills?" I asked.

"I can't get to sleep at night."

"Are you sure that's the only reason?"

Tears flowed down her cheeks. She shook her head. "No," she admitted. "I want to kill myself. I love him so. There's no reason to live anymore." She began to shake convulsively.

If you were the man's wife, would you have told me to give her enough pills to do the job right? Or would you have been willing to let your husband deal with the situation?

After a while, she finally agreed to give me the number of a girl friend who would drive her to the admitting office of a nearby hospital that offered a psychiatric service. There she was treated for her depression and protected from herself. Some "other women" are not so lucky. Shattered love affairs are one of the most frequent causes of suicides.

That is why you cannot afford to interfere when the other woman threatens suicide. Your husband may perceive that the threat is merely a tactic to gain his sympathy. If so, he may take a chance and ignore it. But that must be his choice, not yours. To ease his own conscience, your husband may have to attempt to guide the woman to proper counseling. You may feel ignored while he is helping her. But try to remember that the more you can do to help your husband extricate himself from his relationship with the other woman, the better your chances to patch up the marriage.

My husband is not involved with another woman. He is involved with another man. What should I do?

This is a problem that your husband must work out largely by himself. There is little you can do but try to figure out how it all came about. If he still wants to remain married to you, you must brace yourself for a long, uphill fight. Your marriage probably has less chance of survival than if he had cheated with another woman. Ask yourself if you truly had a marriage in the first place, or if it was merely a convenient living arrangement for him as he tried to work out his own homosexual feelings.

Every one of us has a certain amount of curiosity, interest, or desire when it comes to others of our own sex. We deny these feelings, repress them, reject them, or accept them. The majority of us decide in our adolescence that the opposite sex is far more attractive, and we become practicing heterosexuals. But there is a significant portion of the population that never resolves its conflict with homosexual impulses.

Now that your husband has acknowledged his homosexual feelings, it would be wise for both of you to seek counseling. Only when he begins to understand some of the reasons for his behavior will he be able to decide about his future. But, as I said, the ultimate decision is your husband's alone.

CHAPTER

4

Getting Help

Can my husband and I work out our problems by ourselves, or do we need help?

There is much you can do to help yourselves. Talking the situation over with your husband will bring many of the problems of your marriage into the open. If you are both willing to sit down and talk honestly with one another, you may be surprised how quickly the situation will begin to resolve itself. But it is very easy not to understand fully what is really going on and what you really feel. Sometimes it takes a person who is not involved with the situation to help you clarify your own ideas and understand your own wishes, desires, and goals.

If your husband will not talk with you about your

marriage, you will definitely have to find someone else to discuss it with. You cannot keep it all inside you.

Should I discuss my husband's adultery with my best friend?

If you have a very close friend you can trust, you should talk to her. She knows you well and may be able to give you good advice. At the very least, you will feel better just from confiding in someone. But remember that your friend is not a trained counselor.

Can my minister help?

If you feel comfortable with him, by all means, talk to your clergyman. The majority of people seem to turn first to a priest, minister, or rabbi. Perhaps your husband will go with you to talk, but if you must go alone, do so. Remember that a clergyman's counsel may be colored by his religious viewpoint.

I am Catholic. My priest lectured me against any consideration of divorce. Now I feel trapped. What can I do?

Some people have a tendency to believe that a counselor—especially a clergyman—is always right. The proper role of a counselor, I believe, is to help you make your own decisions, not to make decisions for you. If a counselor offers advice, listen seriously to what he says. Then evaluate his words, consider them, and apply them to your own situation. Remember, he may not always be right.

I am Catholic, too. The priest you talked to is evidently from the old school. He will automatically condemn any suggestion of divorce and berate you for even thinking such "bad" thoughts. I believe that such counseling is unrealistic. Younger priests and some of the older, more enlightened ones receive much more training in marriage counseling today. They have developed a more open attitude toward the problems of modern marriages. So have clergymen of other faiths.

One of my male patients told me that when he first considered having an affair with his neighbor's wife, he sought out a priest for counseling. Early in the discussion, he confessed to the priest that he had been masturbating a lot. The priest, who was old-fashioned in his beliefs, condemned this "sinful" behavior and made the man feel so guilty that he didn't even mention the subject of the woman. He couldn't push the fantasies out of his mind—he only felt more guilty about them. Before long, he actually was having an affair.

I don't really want a divorce. But I have so many questions in my mind about what would happen if my husband moved out. When should I go to see a lawyer?

Many women feel they should not seek legal counsel until they are convinced they want a divorce. On the contrary, I encourage many of my patients to visit a lawyer merely to discuss the alternatives. To make an informed, intelligent decision about the future, you need to know what your legal rights are. You should learn what you can expect in terms of legal fees, alimony, child support, and property division. Just going to a lawyer for advice does not mean you have to take legal action.

Most important, if you have children, you need a basic education in the problems of child custody. You must know how to protect your interests, assuming you wish to keep custody of the children.

My brother-in-law is a lawyer. Should I talk to him?
Generally I would advise against going to any professional counselor who is related to you or who is one of your friends. Because this counselor knows both you and your husband, he may find it difficult to remain objective. You may find it difficult to discuss certain aspects of your problem. But your brother-in-law may be able to recommend another attorney who specializes in marital cases.

How do I find a good lawyer, one I can trust?
If you know of a good tax attorney, for example, you may ask him to recommend a divorce specialist. If one of your friends is divorced, get a recommendation from her. Ask if she was satisfied with the amount of time the lawyer spent on the case, the kinds of questions he asked, and the settlement he was able to work out.

You should shop around for a lawyer. If you meet with one and you just don't like him, you are not required to keep him. Find someone else. Be sure to work with a lawyer who specializes in divorce cases, not someone who handles them as a sideline. If you cannot find such a lawyer by referral, you can always call the local bar association for a list of divorce specialists.

My husband says he has ended his affair, but I suspect

otherwise. Should I hire a private detective to follow him?

Sometimes private detectives are necessary to prove legal points needed to secure a divorce or retain custody of the children. But you should always consult with a lawyer before hiring a private detective. I believe, also, that you should consult with some sort of counselor first. It is important for you to have some idea of what you plan to do with the information once you obtain it (this also goes for reading your husband's mail), and a counselor can help you clarify your thoughts.

When you hire a private detective, you must realize that you are burning the bridge of trust behind you. You are committing yourself to a fight that will probably end in divorce. For a patient named Peggy, this proved to be a big mistake. She was so convinced that her husband was lying about ending his affair that she hired a detective to follow him around. She had found the man through the Yellow Pages and knew nothing about him. He found no evidence against her husband but was so inept that he was spotted. This resulted in a furious argument between Peggy and her husband and very nearly broke up the marriage.

Can my family doctor help me?

If you are blessed with the kind of family doctor who has taken time to talk things over with you in the past, you may wish to discuss the problem with him or her. Many of the younger family-practice specialists are receiving basic training in the treatment of emotional disorders. They are quite capable of helping you and your husband with marital problems, and they are aware of the danger signals that might suggest that you need referral to a mental-health specialist.

Should my husband and I see a marriage counselor? How do I find a good one?

The term *marriage counselor,* used here, is a general one. A variety of people are trained to treat emotional and mental disorders, including psychiatrists, psychologists, and social workers. Marital problems are what bring many patients to them. You can find a marriage counselor by referral from your friends, by calling the local mental health clinic or your county medical society, or by asking your clergyman, lawyer, or family doctor.

Shop around for a good marriage counselor just as you would for a lawyer. Ask yourself three questions:

1. Is this person trained in the techniques of counseling? Unfortunately, in many places, there are little or no licensing requirements. A person can hang out his or her shingle and claim to be in the business of marriage counseling—though he or she may have had no training whatsoever.
2. Is this person licensed or certified and is he or she a member of a professional organization that screens its members? (Such organizations would include the American Psychiatric Association, the American Association of Marriage and Family Counselors, the American Psychological Association, and the National Association of Social Workers).
3. Am I comfortable with this person?

I'm not the one with the problem? Isn't my husband the one who needs counseling?

As I have said, infidelity is a shared problem. Both partners must bear some of the responsibility for the crisis in the marriage and what led to it. Ideally, you and your husband will see a counselor separately and together. If your husband resists the idea, you should go alone, even if it looks as though the marriage is headed for divorce. Counseling can help you prepare for that divorce and for your next personal relationship with a man.

I'm not crazy. Why should I see a psychiatrist?

You don't have to be crazy to see a psychiatrist. In fact, only about fifteen percent of my patients are mentally ill. Most of the others are suffering from anxiety and depression. They are upset and worried, but they can function relatively well when they have to. They are not, by any definition of the word, crazy. But they do have problems that they find hard to resolve by themselves. There should be no shame involved in seeing a psychiatrist or other mental-health professionals.

I've heard that psychiatrists charge up to $50 an hour. How am I going to pay for all of this?

If you have to beg your husband for permission to spend this money, it is an indication that you have not defined your role as an individual very strongly. But realistically, most wives will have to clear such an expense with their husbands. If your husband is willing to pay for counseling, it is a positive sign. He recognizes that there are emotional problems at work within your marriage, and he wants them resolved. It is an even better sign if he is willing to spend money for his own counseling as well as yours.

Many health-insurance plans now cover part of the cost. The remainder is generally a tax-deductible medical expense.

My husband refuses to pay. What can I do about this?

Some of my female patients have successfully asked their husbands whether they would rather pay a marriage counselor or a lawyer. Others have paid for counseling out of their own salaries or taken part-time jobs. Many counselors will make special arrangements with housewives, students, and others who may have difficulty paying. Don't be ashamed to ask. There are community mental-health clinics that charge according to ability to pay.

I feel that my husband's affair is ended. We just want to get our marriage back to normal. Time will heal the wounds. Why do we need counseling?

The answer to this question depends upon your theories of human behavior. I believe that most, if not all, behavior results from emotional causes buried in the past. The fact that your husband cheated, I think, is proof that he is struggling with some emotional problems. If the two of you choose to ignore those problems, you are taking a risk that they will surface once more.

The very fact that you are reading this book shows that you are searching for clues to your husband's (and your own) behavior. Perhaps this book alone will help you solve your marital problems. Perhaps you will need additional counseling. You do not have to make that decision yet. Read on, and try to answer the single most important question about a man who has cheated: Why?

PART II

WHAT WENT WRONG?

CHAPTER
5

Love, Marriage, and Sex

Love is the reason for people.

From our earliest moments, we have a need to know that someone loves us. An infant who is deprived of love will become emotionally disturbed and even die. Therefore, the most important job of a mother and father is to provide the love that their baby craves.

A child's love begins as an intense feeling about his or her mother. Very quickly, father is added to the love. At first, a baby takes love but gives little in return. Soon, however, he begins to give love back. He grins at his parents. He coos softly and reaches out to touch. Baby love radiates from his eyes. The child's ability to give and receive love should gradually mature until he or she is an adult, capable of sharing love with another adult. Ultimately, an adult man or woman should be able to demonstrate love in many ways, one of which is sexual.

But during the course of human development, many things can happen that may slow—or stop—the maturation process. To resolve your marriage crisis, you must try to measure the quality of love you have for one another. Is there love in your marriage? Is it mature? How is it demonstrated? Does the quality of your sex life indicate your love for one another?

My husband never says, "I love you." Does that mean he doesn't?

Saying "I love you" means very little by itself. It's nice to hear the words once in awhile, but they are not necessary if love is really being demonstrated. The immature person who must be constantly reassured by words is like a child who wants a lollipop *right now.*

One of my female patients who had successfully undergone psychotherapy came back to see me years later, upset and crying. "Nobody loves me," she sobbed. "Even the kids don't know I exist unless dinner isn't ready on time."

"Do you think your husband loves you?" I asked.

"I don't know. He just goes about his work. He doesn't seem to notice when I've cleaned the house. He never sees that his bureau is filled with fresh shirts. I'm just a maid."

"Do the kids ever bring their friends home for dinner?"

She nodded.

"Does your husband ever bring anyone home from the office?"

"Uh huh. He likes me to make lasagna for them."

"Well, it seems to me that your children and your husband are proud of your home and your cooking. They don't hesitate to bring their friends over. What more testimony do you need?"

She dried her tears. Gently I reminded her about her previous sessions when we had tried to increase her sense of self-worth. She had matured a lot during those sessions, and now she simply needed to think carefully about them again. She had forgotten to look for the real testimonies of love—the quiet ones.

Should I ask my husband if he loves me?

Once in awhile, perhaps, when you are feeling particularly insecure, it is all right to ask. But be careful not to nag him constantly with the question. Then his expected answer will become meaningless. Try to look for the unspoken answer to the unspoken question.

Let me illustrate what I mean by relating one of my own experiences. Late one afternoon, shortly before I was due to fly to Atlanta for a professional meeting, I noticed spots on my favorite palm. I had nurtured it for years, and I felt that part of me would die if the plant died. I called the garden shop immediately, and the clerk recommended a spray. Bart was in the den watching the news when I rushed in with the palm. He could see I was upset, because I didn't have time both to spray the plant and to catch my plane. Without a moment's hesitation, he took the plant and assured me he would care for it right away. He could have waited. He could have scoffed at my concern. But he sensed how important it was to me, got up from his comfortable chair, and went to attend to the plant.

Now, when I look at it thriving in the afternoon sunshine, I feel good about him. The plant says "I love you" more eloquently than he could have expressed it by putting his feelings into words.

I always dreamed of having a perfect marriage. Now that my husband has cheated, my dreams are shattered. Will I ever be happy with something less than perfect?

You have to be, for no marriage can be perfect. You must learn how to love an imperfect man. Your question indicates that you may be one of those women who is in love with love, or in love with the *idea* of marriage more than with your husband. You may have been taught from your earliest moments that marriage will bring you incomparable bliss. You may not care whom you are married to, as long as you are married. Of course, the bliss is simply not there, and then the problems begin.

When a patient named Ed described his home to me, he provided a telltale clue as to what his wife Alice expected from her marriage. "She is a perfectionist in an apron," Ed complained. Everything had to be in place at all times. Every nook and cranny had to be dusted, swept, washed, and/or sanitized. Cleanliness is healthy, but obsession with it is not. A woman's abnormal compulsion to keep her home spotless indicates that she may also expect a perfect marriage. Ed, not a neat man by nature, could never hope to live up to her expectations completely.

Certainly the woman who has made her marriage her whole life will feel a tremendous sense of failure if she doesn't do a perfect job. And if her husband's needs are incompatible with her expectations, she will suffer greatly.

Should we have tried living together before we were married?

Living together is in vogue. It is an experiment with a different life-style in our endless search to improve human relations. I would be happy if it eventually proved to be more effective than our present marriage customs. But I don't believe that will be the case.

Many people will disagree with me, but I believe your relationship has a better chance of survival if you are willing to take the risk of making the union legally binding. A large number of couples today are unwilling to make that commitment. In my opinion, this sets them up for failure. They begin life together with the idea that if it doesn't work out, they can always run away. When mature people decide to leave their parents and establish their own life together, I believe they will want to make the break complete—and official. Living with another human being is not easy. It takes work. Because marriage strengthens their ties, it forces a couple to work harder in order to succeed.

Even if a couple lives together successfully beforehand, I don't believe it guarantees a successful marriage. A legal commitment is really the only way to test the depths of your relationship.

Sometimes I feel that I could get along just as well without my husband. Does this mean I should consider a divorce?

Perhaps it does. Ideally, a marriage should be a situation in which two whole, integrated people try to capitalize on and complement each other's strengths. Therefore, your marriage should result in a union that is stronger than either of you alone. If you feel you could probably function better without your husband, you may not need to be married to him.

I found this to be the case with a patient named Ann. She is a research chemist, a professional woman. She does not need her husband to take her hand and walk her in and out of each day. She has her own source of income. Of course, she would like to have a husband who loved her and could make her life happier. She had a fantasy of that sort of relationship when she married Allen. When Allen turned out to be a homosexual, Ann was shocked and hurt. But over the course of a few months of counseling, she realized that she didn't need him. She could survive on her own. The divorce hurt, but she emerged from it with a new sense of independence and strength.

We will discuss this subject more fully in a later chapter.

My husband and I married when we were still in our teens. Did that doom us to failure?

Not necessarily. The chance for success in any marriage seems to depend upon the degree of maturity each person brings to the partnership. Some eighteen-year-olds are as mature as twenty-four-year olds, but most are not. If a couple in their late teens decide to get married, they should at least have reached the level of maturity for their age. If they have, and if both continue to grow as individuals and as a couple and work at their marriage, the chances for success are good.

On the other hand, the husband of one of my patients is thirty-five years old, but he acts like a rebellious teenager. He dislikes the idea of his wife trying to take away any of his fun. He doesn't think he should have to tell her where he is going and when he will be home. New clothes, motorcycles, or boats—whatever turns him on at the moment—are what he has to have, regardless of the bills that might have to be paid in the future. Not surprisingly, he has been cheating on his wife for years.

My husband's career has blossomed. His life is exciting. He travels a lot and meets interesting people, many of them women. I stay home, change diapers, and take care of the house. Is there any hope for us when we seem to have grown so far apart?

Hope depends upon how ready, willing, and able you are to begin to change your own life. The woman who says she is satisfied with staying home and changing diapers may or may not be telling the truth. If she is, and her husband's very different life is causing problems, then the marriage may not last. But often a woman says she is happy to remain at home only because she feels too inadequate, threatened, and dependent to live as active a life as her husband. In such cases, frustrations build in both husband and wife that sometimes burst out in adultery. There is hope for the marriage only if this frustrated woman can finally begin to be honest with herself and consider doing something about her situation. When a woman develops her own interests and thereby becomes an interesting person in her own right, she will be less demanding of her husband. And when that happens, love is often rekindled. Wives who ask for less of their husbands often get more.

I think sex is too available today. Wasn't that a big factor in my husband's cheating?

Possibly, because he may feel as if he's missed out on something. But a lot of cheating also took place back in the days when sex was a taboo subject in America. Now the pendulum has swung in the opposite direction, and we are surrounded by sex. It is difficult to say whether cheating has increased. But I believe that the sexual revolution is better than puritanism (if we had to make a choice), even though it sometimes results in abuses. The expression of sex seems to be more beneficial than the total repression of one of life's most basic needs.

Naturally we are concerned about rapes, sex murders, and public lewdness. But there are far fewer sex-related crimes than cases of suicide, drug abuse, nervous breakdown, wife- and child-beating, impotence, and frigidity —many of which are due to the guilt people suffer because of the guilt from our society's past puritanical attitudes toward sex.

The healthy individual seems to be the one who can strike a balance between the extremes.

Why does sex cause such problems?

Because we are human beings. Without the frontal cortex of the brain (which makes us human), we would automatically enjoy having our sexual organs stimulated by any man, woman, child, animal, plant, or inanimate object. And we would feel no guilt. But this is a concept that the frontal cortex of the brain has difficulty coping with. We are constantly in the midst of a battle between the nerve endings of our sex organs and the human considerations within our brains. This conflict shows up in my office (and the offices of all other psychiatrists) as a wide variety of sexual problems. When partners have sexual disagreements, they are usually extremely frustrated. Often this frustration results in an attempt to find a new sex partner. Part of determining what went wrong with your marriage involves identifying any sex problems that exist.

What is the most common sex problem?

Probably frigidity.

What causes frigidity?

When a woman is unable to reach orgasm, the cause is usually psychological. But before a psychiatrist can assume this, he or she should send the patient to her family doctor for a complete examination to be sure there is no organic cause. Though this is not usually the case, frigidity can be caused by displacement of the uterus, anemia, diabetes, and several other conditions.

Once physical problems are eliminated, we begin to look for psychological ones. (Sometimes the problem is due to a combination of physical and psychological causes.) Often frigidity arises out of a woman's lack of understanding of her sexual capabilities. For years, she simply submits to her husband's sexual techniques, even though they may do little to please her. Only recently have women even begun to realize their right to orgasm. Frigidity may arise from faulty sex education, a poor attitude toward men, a lack of self-confidence, or past sexual mistreatment.

Why is frigidity in women more prevalent than impotence in men?

The primary reason is that, unlike men, women can fake orgasm and thus keep their problem a secret. All too often a woman, supposedly living in an age when sexual attitudes have become liberated, watches her satisfied husband roll over and go to sleep while she lies awake, frustrated and angry.

A patient named Irene was typical. She probably should have received an Academy Award for her acting in bed. She didn't want to hurt her husband Steve's feelings by making him appear inadequate. But he sensed the problem, even though he didn't discuss it with her. Instead, he found a girl friend. Irene had suffered for years through unenjoyable sex, pretending all the time to come to fulfillment. Now she felt rejected. She built up a volcano of anger toward Steve that erupted in my office one day.

"He should know I'm pretending!" she argued.

"How? He can't read your mind?"

"Men know . . . Don't they?"

"Irene, one of the first places to begin to be honest with him is in bed. When Steve is at the height of orgasm, he becomes a very selfish person—rightfully so. At that particular moment, he doesn't know and doesn't really care what is happening to you. That's what you would be doing if you reached orgasm. You would be thinking of your own pleasure. He hopes you are experiencing enjoyment, but he is enjoying a primarily self-centered moment. A man does not automatically know how to please a woman. If you've been pretending that you are pleased, you should not blame him for your remaining frustrated."

"What do I do?"

"Well, I would say the first thing would be to recognize that you are pretending. Then we can begin to work to find out why you are unable to come to an orgasm. Maybe the fault lies with Steve's sexual technique. Or maybe it really stems from your background."

Overcoming frigidity can be a difficult task, but it is necessary if you are to have a happy sex life. If you are pretending, you are short-changing yourself. Life is too short to play that game.

How can I overcome frigidity?

There is no easy answer. You should discuss it first with your gynecologist and then with your husband. If, however, you feel uneasy about discussing your frigidity with your husband, you may wish to seek professional counseling beforehand. Perhaps when you understand your own problem better, you will be able to talk to your husband about it without hurting his ego.

Intercourse is painful for me. What is wrong?

Sometimes this pain is caused by a physical condition, but usually it is not. When the cause is psychological, we call the condition vaginismus. If a woman is emotionally ready for sex, the thin muscles that line the vaginal opening are relaxed and lubricated by the secretion from the vaginal glands. But if her mind says, "No!" the muscles may contract so tightly that entrance becomes difficult. The glands fail to secrete. It is little wonder that intercourse hurts.

You probably have found ways of avoiding the pain. You might have learned to pick a fight with your husband just before bedtime. Or you may be in the habit of going to bed earlier than he. Women who suffer from vaginismus learn to shun any advance that might ultimately lead to sex, and they often drive their husbands to another woman's bed.

You should stop hiding the problem from your husband. Then you should talk to your gynecologist about it.

My husband usually experiences orgasm very quickly—often in less than a minute. It is hard for me to become aroused in such a short time. Is this my problem or his?

It is a problem for both of you, since sex is supposed to be a shared experience. But premature ejaculation is basically a male problem. It is one of the few sexual disorders that does not have a possible physical cause—the cause is *always* psychological. Most frequently it is caused by the man's concern over how well he will perform. This becomes magnified if he is aware that his partner is having difficulty achieving orgasm. The man takes the entire blame for this, tries harder to perform, and fails.

Many of my patients have unsatisfactory sex lives

because the woman is frigid and the man suffers from premature ejaculation. If they are afraid to bring their difficulties into the open, those difficulties usually become worse. Before long, one or both of them decides to find out whether they would be more compatible with someone else.

What are other causes of premature ejaculation?

There are a variety of causes, including other, nonsexual problems between the partners, such as how to spend money, how to discipline the children, conflicts with in-laws, death of a child or parent, bankruptcy, terminal illness. Sometimes the causes are completely unconscious, such as incestual desires, fear of castration, or a feeling that sex is sinful.

What can be done about premature ejaculation?

Any amount of chiding or criticism will only make matters worse. This can be a terribly humiliating condition for a man. If it persists, both partners will require sexual and psychological counseling. While the man is convinced that it is his problem, in reality, the woman may be doing much to reinforce it.

Often my husband is unable to sustain an erection. What is causing this problem?

There are a variety of physical and emotional causes of impotence. The physical ones include (but are not limited to) high blood pressure, diabetes, alcoholism, multiple sclerosis, leukemia, prostate gland disease, spinal disease, thyroid gland dysfunction, and certain intestinal and spinal surgical procedures. The emotional causes of impotence are similar to those responsible for other sexual problems.

Any man may suffer from occasional impotence. But if the condition lasts longer than he and his wife can endure, then he should first see a doctor to rule out a physical cause. If none can be found, they both should seek professional help.

My husband admitted to me that he masturbates frequently. Could this have led to his affair?

Excessive masturbation is often a form of sexual overindulgence. It can satisfy one's hunger just enough to take the edge off the appetite, so that sex with one's partner may be postponed or replaced. It may indicate that your husband is not satisfied with your sex life together, and thus it could have contributed to his affair.

A man who is anxious to avoid foreplay may turn to masturbation. Sometimes he is too impatient to wait for his partner. Or she may not be able to respond to his caressing, so that he finds more pleasure in masturbation. It is also sometimes used as a pleasant escape from reality, or even as a sleeping pill. Excessive masturbation can spoil healthy sexual response, just as the chronic use of laxatives promotes a lazy bowel, or eating too much leads to obesity, or drinking too much leads to alcoholism.

My husband wants sex all the time. Should I give in to him, even though I don't enjoy having sex as often as he does?

All men take pride in their virility, but some must constantly attempt to be superstuds. It is hard to say what is normal sexual performance, but sexual overindulgence indicates some sort of emotional problem. It is particularly difficult for the partner who is supposed to live up to the demands of an unhealthy appetite.

A patient once complained to me that her husband had developed a sudden need for a lunchtime "quickie." Every day he raced home at noon and dragged her off to bed. If a friend was visiting, he would tell her rudely to leave because he "needed" his wife. Embarrassed and angry, the woman nevertheless continued to submit. She reasoned that if she didn't, her husband would find someone else. When she finally persuaded him to come to see me, he admitted that he was also masturbating two or three times a day. Fortunately, he agreed to continue with therapy and their problems were resolved when he understood the reasons for his behavior and decided to try to change.

I confess I must be the female equivalent of a superstud. I have an almost constant need for sex, and over the years, I have had numerous affairs without my husband's knowledge. What is wrong with me?

In a woman, sexual overindulgence is usually called nymphomania. But whether in a man or woman, it is usually caused by one of three things:

1. *Premature ejaculation, impotence, or the fear of impotence in men; frigidity in women.* Since they are unable to perform as well as they feel they should, indi-

viduals who have this problem search endlessly for the perfect sexual situation. After each failure, they usually blame the situation or the partner.

2. *Basic feelings of inadequacy.* Constant sex with a variety of partners gives those who feel deficient a reaffirmation of their sexual desirability.

3. *Desire for escape.* Some people use sex the way others use alcohol, drugs, or food. Sex for them is a temporary, pleasurable release from the tensions of life.

My husband and I have had our most ardent sessions of lovemaking right after our most brutal fights. Is this normal?

This may be an indication of a sadomasochistic relationship. Wife- and husband-beating are critical problems today. Thousands of men and women are regularly treated in the emergency rooms of hospitals after their spouses beat them up. It happens again and again, police call after police call, separation after separation. Still the injured spouse takes the other back. Why? The most common reason given is, "For the sake of the children." But what kind of children are you raising if you give them a constant show of unmerciful domestic violence?

The sad fact of the matter is that many couples enjoy this game. The one who does the beating is the sadist; the victim is the masochist. The key to diagnosing this perversion is simple. When there is a history of constant physical or verbal abuse and the husband and wife still manage to maintain a good sex life together, they usually have a sadomasochistic relationship. They need psychiatric help before one of them kills or permanently injures the other, as well as "for the sake of the kids."

Why do my husband and I seem to have so much difficulty pleasing one another in bed?

If you could marry yourself, you would be sexually compatible. But when you married another human being, each of you brought to the marriage a different set of preferences, problems and hang-ups. It continually amazes me that so many couples rarely, if ever, discuss their sex lives. This refusal to talk about such a critical subject is one of the main reasons you have difficulty pleasing one another.

Why does sex make me feel so guilty?

The attitudes you learned from your parents are usually the cause. And, all too often, religion has also made a large contribution. Religion plays a very important role in the lives of many people. It even influences those who profess not to have it. In my work with patients, I have found that those who have some belief in a strength outside themselves seem to have a little more of the "something" that is needed to cope with periods of overwhelming stress.

Unfortunately, however, religious precepts have generally been taught in a destructive, sexually repressive manner. Too much guilt has been placed upon people in an attempt to restrict thoughts, feelings, and behavior that are really very human. Almost all children raised in our society develop guilt feelings about masturbation. Lust is classified in Christianity as one of the seven deadly sins, even if it is only a fleeting thought. Certain sexual methods, even when used by a married man and woman, are "bad."

I believe that when one human being places a burden

of guilt upon another human being, it is far more sinful than any sexual misconduct. Guilt is the deadliest of all psychological sins. It is the basis for most of the problems that my patients have. When the clergy and others use the guilt tactic to influence behavior, they create hell on earth for others.

But there are changes going on. Clergymen are beginning to wake up to the realities of sex and are changing their counsel. But it will take generations to remove the negative effects of past education. I am no libertine, but it seems to me that we must stop teaching children to fear a God who will punish them not only for wrong deeds, but for even thinking about wrong deeds. We must start teaching them to love a God who, because of His goodness, will understand that no human being is perfect and that none of us has all the answers to his problems.

If God didn't want us to be sexual, why did He give us all those erogenous zones?

What sexual variations are healthy between two people?

A variety of sexual positions, oral and anal sex, and all manner of variations in sexual foreplay can be healthy expressions between a man and a woman, if they decide together that they enjoy them. Too many women, I believe, feel it is the man's responsibility to provide that variety. There are a lot of movements a woman can make that will heighten the enjoyment for both herself and her husband.

How do I discover those movements?

You experiment with your husband. Sex is like dining out. When you and your husband decide that you are hungry and that you would like to go out for dinner, you must choose a restaurant together. Sometimes your husband may want a thick, juicy steak while you could settle for a chef's salad. Maybe you like Chinese food and he likes Italian. Sometimes you might both be in the mood for a quick hamburger. You have to compromise. Sex offers a whole smorgasbord of possibilities. Unless you sample them, you will not know what you like and dislike.

My husband likes to perform oral sex on me and wants me to do the same for him, but it makes me feel dirty. Why?

Most adult Americans today were raised with a repressive attitude toward sex. Mother, and often Father, made it clear that there was something dirty about it. This set up an immediate conflict. You knew that you felt good when you touched your sexual organs, but that they were considered unclean even if you had just taken a bath. Usually you grew to believe that the pleasurable feeling was morally dirty, also. Despite the new sexual openness, this belief still persists. One of the ways to rid yourself of it is to understand that it stems from overly protective training.

One of my patients just could not bring herself to perform oral sex on her husband, no matter how hard she tried. After many sessions with her, it became clear that she was afraid of germs on her husband's penis. I pointed out that there were as many—if not more—germs in her mouth than on his penis, but this didn't seem to help. Slowly, over several months of therapy, she began to understand what the word *germ* meant to her. Her mother had taught her to wash her body several times a day, so that now a tolerance of any "germ" felt like a betrayal of Mother. She also realized that as a result of her strict religious training, she equated the word *germ* with sin.

This patient did not change overnight. However, once she was aware of her attitudes, she could begin to compartmentalize them. In a sense, one part of her could laugh at the irrational feelings of another part. After a time, she learned to tolerate oral sex—and now she is beginning to enjoy it.

My husband told me he feels like a failure when I don't climax at the same time he does. That's why he says he wanted to try another woman. Is he being realistic?

No. Mutual orgasm is not necessary for sexual fulfillment. Many men, especially when they are first married, cannot prolong an erection. For various reasons, a man who is just beginning his sex life is not able to postpone his own release long enough to fulfill his wife. The woman often cannot accept the fact that he can bring her to orgasm in any other manner. She remains unfulfilled, and he is disappointed with his own performance.

I have a hard time reaching orgasm. What should we do?

Your husband needs to learn how to give you pleasure. But first you yourself need to know what feels best. Once you find that out by reading about your body and exploring your own body, and by allowing your husband to fondle you in a variety of ways, you must tell or show him what to do. If you are unable to reach orgasm despite both your efforts, the problem lies much deeper than technique and requires professional help.

Often, when I am having sex with my husband, I fantasize about other men. Does this make me unusual?

Not at all. To be aroused by a sexual partner, you must like him—or at least be able to fantasize a more positive someone or something. Your body cannot be turned on if your mind is turned off. Ideally, your thoughts will be on your partner and the pleasure that is taking place. But second best, sexually speaking, is to be able to enjoy the sex regardless of the fantasies that are floating around in your mind.

Should I tell my husband about my fantasies?

I do not advocate that you and your husband tell each other everything. If you were both perfect, you could handle it. While you should respect the privacy of each other's minds, you should also be willing to share your fantasy life *selectively* with your husband. You can learn to share certain sexual fantasies as long as you are sure they will not threaten him.

And you must both remember to make a sharp distinction between what is fantasy and what is reality.

Is sex the most important thing in my husband's life?

No. Quite simply, the most important part of any man's life is his job. He views himself as the breadwinner. Right or wrong, he tends to base his estimate of self-worth on the progress of his career. Career problems are one of the most frequent causes of sexual problems, rather than vice versa. If a man's job is not going well, he may use sex to relieve his frustrations. Or he may not be able to perform sexually at all.

There are many difficulties in a man's life that may cause him to feel inadequate, unloved, or bored. Our culture often teaches—erroneously, I believe—that a sexual adventure may solve these problems. It is quite possible that your husband cheated in an attempt to solve inner troubles that may seem unrelated to sex. Now is the time to search for those anxieties.

CHAPTER

6

Clues from the Past

My husband complains that I don't understand him. How can I begin to do so?

Understanding someone else takes time. First you must learn to understand yourself. Do you really know who you are? Do you really know your husband? To understand an individual in his present emotional state, you must learn about his past—the events that molded him into the person he now is. This is perhaps the most neglected part of marriage—attempting to comprehend your partner's background, and sharing your own with him. We all have skeletons in our closet, and it is often painful to share those secrets with someone else. But that is the only way to begin to see how and where your husband has received his strengths and weaknesses. It is the way to begin to understand him, yourself, and why all this happened.

How can I get my husband to talk about his past?

Try a discussion like this: "Honey, we've worked long and hard for everything that we have. I don't want to throw it away. I want to understand what went wrong in our marriage, to see in what way I have contributed to it. I feel we both contributed to the problems. Maybe if we understand more about each other, we'll have a better relationship. It's about time we sat down and got to know one another."

Don't be discouraged if your husband immediately says no. Give him some time to think about it. He may storm out the door in anger, but while he is out blowing off steam, the truth of your words may begin to sink in. If he never does accept your invitation, the outlook for the marriage is poor. But you will feel better for having tried. You will also be on the road to a better understanding of yourself, which you will need if you are to face the next years alone. And you will be better prepared to build a more healthy relationship next time.

But there is a good chance your husband will respond. If so, you must both remember that what is important is not really your "marriage." That is merely a legal binding upon your relationship. It is the relationship itself that is important—more important than the adultery that disrupted it—and your relationship, of course, began some time prior to your wedding. When you look back over the months and years that you knew your future husband before marriage, you will pick up clues as to what went wrong.

The following is a list of questions you should have asked yourself about your husband before you married him. Try to think back to the time of your engagement and evaluate how ready he was to marry. If you could have spotted many of these traits in him, you would have known that the marriage was headed for trouble. Understanding them now will help you decide about the future.

- *Did he have exaggerated personality traits?* Did he suffer frequent periods of depression? Was he compulsively clean? A perfectionist? Too demanding of others? Did he lie to you repeatedly, or at least withhold information from you? Was he compelled to perform exciting but dangerous acts, such as unnecessary chances with his car, an unusual interest in fires, or sadistic or masochistic sexual practices? Did he hit you? Was he unable to express himself well? Was he able to bear responsibility when things went wrong (or did he always blame other people or circumstances)? Was he overly possessive of you, assuming that if you wanted a night for yourself, you would be out looking for another man?
- *Did his family have exaggerated personality traits?* Was there a family history of depression, suicide, alcoholism, drug abuse, or mental illness? Did they make harsh demands on his time even though he was supposed to be separating from them? Is there a history of divorce and separation in his family? What realistic

demands did his family make on him that would become *your* problem, too, such as caring for an ill or elderly parent?

• *Did he fail to have a career goal, or was that goal incompatible with your own image of the husband and life-style you wanted?* Did he change jobs frequently? Did he spend too much time at work or study? Did he find it difficult to share with you his frustrations and fears about his career?

• *Did he have difficulty establishing a one-to-one relationship with you?* Did he always seem to need other people around at the same time he was with you? Did you feel as though you were competing with his best friend for attention? Did he find it necessary to befriend people much younger than himself (or much older)? Was he able both to give and take in your relationship? Did his actions show that he found children a bother?

• *Did he have difficulty coping with problems?* Was he a procrastinator? A worrywart? Did he tend to escape from his problems by abusing alcohol, drugs, sleep, food, friends, or sex? Did he learn from his past experiences, or did he make the same mistakes again and again? How flexible was he in dealing with the unexpected?

• *Did he have no interest in extracurricular activities?* Did he lack hobbies (other than sex and drinking)? Did he only want to sit around and watch television? Was he reluctant to take a train or airplane anywhere? Or did he overdo his hobbies? Did he spend too much time and money on them? Did you feel as though you were in competition with his hobbies? Did you share an interest in his hobbies?

• *If he was married before, how sensible was his attitude about his first failure?* Did he refuse to share any of the responsibility for the breakup of his previous marriage? Or did he take all the blame? Is he still involved with his ex-wife? Did he refuse to discuss the problems of his first marriage with you? Did he spend too little time with his children? Or did he overindulge them? Did he demand that you love them like your own? Did he constantly compare you with his first wife?

• *Did he have a healthy attitude toward sex?* Was he so inexperienced that he had never seriously "petted"? Did he too quickly accept your protests that he slow down and wait a bit until marriage? Did he show disrespect for your sexual attitudes and desires? If you had more previous sexual experiences than he, did he hold that against you? Did he refuse to let you teach him? Did he allow variety in sexual practices, or did he only believe in sexual intercourse done one way? Was he unwilling to compromise with you on your mutual sexual desires?

Now look at your own experiences in those traumatic years of dating, and ask yourself these questions:

• *How honest were you?* Each of us has a variety of masks that we wear throughout the day. Much like the old theater performers who changed from a happy mask to a tragic one to fit the particular mood of a play, we change our masks to relate to different people. But when a woman wants to build a lasting, loving relationship with a man, she must take off her masks. Your husband should be the one human being, above all, who knows you as you really are, and vice versa.

From the very beginning of their dating relationship, Sally hid her true feelings from Jerry. Jerry would show up at ten o'clock when he was supposed to pick Sally up at eight. He always had some excuse, such as, "I got tied up with the boys and didn't want them to think I was henpecked, so I didn't call." Although she should have told him to get lost, Sally always gave in to the box of candy or the gift of flowers he would bring as a peace offering. She hid her anger, melted into his arms, and forgave him. She always figured that once they were married, she could change him.

I know this sounds trite, but honesty really is the best policy in human relationships. With it, you and your husband can relax and enjoy each other. Without it, you are always on guard. Chances are that if you were not honest with each other in the very beginning, you will find it almost impossible to be so today.

• *How mature were you when the two of you began dating each other?* Both Sally and Jerry were acting childishly. Jerry was still too much of an adolescent to separate himself from his peer group. He had to spend time with the boys. Sally, for her part, reacted like a little girl who could be bought off with trinkets. She still had the starry-eyed teenager's vision of marriage in which two imperfect people suddenly become perfect due to the magical transforming powers of love.

Too often a young bride is not emotionally ready to live her own life. She falls in love with a man merely because she knows she has to leave home soon and wants someone to take the place of her parents. She likes the feeling of being protected and cared for. She somehow never becomes capable of going shopping alone, finding her own seat in a theater, or driving through the city. Were you searching for a lover or a parent when you met you future husband?

• *How much dating experience did you have?* "My momma told me," says an old popular song, "you better shop around." It is generally a danger signal when I meet a husband and wife who only dated each other. High-school sweethearts who always "went steady" and then got married are often like children who must have peanut butter and jelly for lunch because they have never tried cheese, lettuce, and tomato. Variety is necessary in dating if a woman is to have a reasonable idea of the kind of man she wants to marry.

Another advantage of dating different men is that it gives you the ability to handle rejection. Learning how to reject or say no and how to be rejected is a necessary part of the growing-up process. Those painful teenage tears may seem like the end, but they are really the beginning of an important stage of emotional development. Sometimes a man and woman will marry simply to avoid the pain of rejecting one another.

• *How much sexual experience did you have before marriage?* Remember the confusion about whether you should go "all the way"? I am not an advocate of premarital sex. But I am not a prude, either. I don't believe that a person necessarily has to try out sex before marriage, particularly if it will go against her conscience, but at the very least, she should be moving toward a more fulfilling sexual relationship as marriage approaches. Sexual maturity does not come suddenly in one explosive experience.

Doug always accepted the fact that Barbara was determined to be a virgin on their wedding night. And since they couldn't go all the way, he reasoned, why bother with too much petting? Looking back on their experience today, Barbara remembers that Doug never became amorous unless he had had a few drinks. At the time, she respected his behavior. Now that Doug has admitted he is a homosexual, Barbara realizes that she should have seen the warning signs.

A low level of sexual experience prior to marriage does not automatically indicate homosexuality or other serious problems. But if, as the wedding day approached, one or the other of you resisted the advance of sexual practices, the resistance was a sign that some sort of hang-up would surface later.

But promiscuous sexual behavior before marriage can also be a danger signal. It indicates that an individual has difficulty committing himself or herself to another person.

There is a tendency now for men and women to try out sex with one another before marriage in order to test their sexual compatibility. My feelings about this are mixed. If the couple enjoy a free and easy attitude about sex, fine. But many people are still raised with a heritage of guilt about premarital sex. That feeling of guilt—not the sex act itself—can produce a serious emotional hangover. Before you jump into bed, you must be confident that you can handle whatever amount of guilt—if any—will result.

One of my cases demonstrates that premarital sex between an engaged couple does not guarantee compatibility. The patient who came to me was the husband. Ken had met his present wife Judy when both were in the process of getting divorced from their first spouses. They fell in love. Unable to wait until their divorces were final, they began to live together. They seemed to get along well, and their sex life was good.

Ken and Judy let their situation drag on. Seven years after they began living together, Ken was still not divorced from his first wife. Their common-law relationship might have continued peacefully, except for the pressure of relatives on both sides of the family. No social occasion went by without some reference to the couple "living in sin." Finally Ken gave in. He divorced his first wife and married Judy.

Two weeks later Ken found himself unable to sustain an erection for more than a few minutes. After several sessions of therapy, it became clear that he was afraid of the responsibilities that go along with the commitment of marriage. This anxiety was part of the difficulty with his first marriage. Now that he found himself burdened with the duties of another marriage (though, in effect, nothing had changed about his relationship with Judy), he became fearful again. The fear showed up as a sex problem. As he came to realize the cause, he was able to overcome it.

• *How much did you know about each other's past?* Sometimes a woman tends to be obsessive about learning the details of her husband's premarital sex life. Such an interest indicates she is comparing herself against the other women—and probably lacks self-confidence.

But, more frequently, people want to know little or nothing about the early life of a prospective spouse. Yet the details of growing up—family traits, health history, fantasies, sex education, religious experience, and all the other emotional bumps and bruises of childhood are the keys to personality—the things that make each of us unique.

• *Did you share your own background with him?* Did you ask about his? One danger signal is a person's refusal to talk about the past, or a denial of the existence of many memories. That probably indicates that growing up was an experience so traumatic that the memories are still painful.

There is no better time than the present to face the past. Something has gone wrong with your marriage. The adultery that took place (whether committed by your husband or yourself) is a sign that it is time for some changes. Pressures have built up within the marriage and have blown the lid off what you may have thought was your happy home. Now that you both clearly realize that there are serious problems, you must do your best to identify them.

CHAPTER 7

Kathy and Larry

The next three chapters present detailed histories from my casebook, showing how three very different couples tried to cope with adultery in their marriages. (The cases are somewhat disguised, but they are faithful to reality.) Each of these cases is presented here to illustrate various reasons cheating occurs. Read carefully and look for clues that will help with your own marital problems.

It was Larry who came to me first. He was a bright young lawyer, twenty-nine years old, tall and lanky. He complained of not feeling "like his old self." He said he found it harder and harder to get up in the mornings and go to work. At night, it took him hours to fall asleep, and when he finally did, he had troublesome dreams. Larry felt he was "burning out" at a very early age.

As he spoke, he shifted his position in the chair frequently and seemed ready to jump up and leave my office at any moment. His words poured out in a staccato beat. His biggest worry, he said, was that his clients would leave his fledgling law practice because he no longer had the energy to work hard for them. But he admitted that he frequently stayed late at the office or went there on weekends in a frantic attempt to find just one more court ruling to corroborate his position. Although he won most of his cases, Larry often had difficulty collecting the fees. He didn't want to press his clients for money because of a feeling that he had let them down—even when he won. He wanted me to help him regain his energy and his zest for living.

"With all of this worry about your work, I wonder what effect it is having on your marriage," I commented. Larry looked at me with disbelief. Then he began to tell me about his real problem.

He and Kathy, who worked as a computer operator, had been married six years and had no children. "She's such a good, hard-working wife," Larry said. "She gets up early in the morning and tends to the housework before leaving for her office. In the afternoon, she rushes home and always has dinner waiting for me. In the evening, she works hard to keep the house spotless. She's perfect. She even irons my socks!"

I waited quietly and patiently. Soon Larry started to talk more freely. "There's this woman at the office," he said. "She's . . . she's taking a year off college to work with us . . . to see if she really wants to be a lawyer. I've been . . . uh . . . thinking a lot about her. She's got beautiful blonde hair. I dream about her often and I wake up with a hard-on. One night when we were working late at the office . . . just the two of us . . . we made love. I feel so bad about this. I've never been unfaithful to Kathy before. I really feel guilty. But I can't get my mind off Beth. I even get hot flashes when I first see her in the morning. I can't work around her."

"Do you love her?"

"I don't know."

"Do you love Kathy?"

"I . . . don't know that either. I'm scared. I don't even want to think about divorce."

"Why?"

"My parents are Catholic. Dad would disown me."

"Does Kathy suspect that something is wrong?"

"Yes. She knows I've been tired and irritable. She's tried to talk with me about it, but I don't know what to say. I can't tell her about Beth. It would kill her."

Larry lapsed into silence. I waited again for him to continue. "I've just . . . got to tell someone. I guess that's why I came to see you," he said.

"Do you really think you can keep it from her forever?"

"I don't know. I thought I could. But it's tearing me up inside."

One week later Larry came back for his second session. He was pale and haggard-looking. But he was calmer than he had been during our first meeting.

"I told Kathy," he announced. A great weight seemed to lift off his shoulders. "It wasn't easy. I sat down with her a couple nights ago and told her I wanted to talk. She was nervous—she knew it was going to be a very serious talk. I don't know how I did it but I blurted it out. God! It was one of the hardest things I've ever done in my life."

"How did she react?"

"At first, she just stared at me. Big tears started rolling down her cheeks. She didn't say a word. She let me finish my story. Then she said she had known something was wrong. She had wondered about another woman, but she'd been so afraid to ask me. She said she needed time to think, that her whole world was spinning. She asked me if I would sleep in a motel that night."

"Did she raise her voice?"

"No. Her mother was asleep upstairs. But Kathy's not the kind to fight like that anyway. She took it rather well, I thought. I know it hurt her very badly. I wanted to reach out and touch her, but she pulled away from me. After a while, she just ran upstairs crying. I packed a few things and went away for the night."

"Are you still living somewhere else?"

"No. I was in the motel just that one night. Kathy called me at the office the next day. She said she was still very confused and it would take her a long time to figure things out. But she asked if I wanted to come back home. She'd lied to her mother—told her that I had to go out of town on business. She was too embarrassed to tell her the truth. Anyway, she said she would like it if I'd come home while we tried to figure out what to do. Then . . ." he said, his voice cracking, "she said she loved me."

Larry cried. He sat across from me, his shoulders heaving. I waited for him to compose himself. "What are we going to do?" he wailed.

"What would you like to do?"

"I don't know. It's all so confusing. Sometimes I think I want to patch things up with Kathy and sometimes I think I'm outgrowing her and the best thing to do is split. How do I know which is the real feeling?"

"They're both real feelings. But you have to decide which is stronger, and which is better for you . . . and for Kathy."

"How do I do that?"

"I think you both need to understand a little better why all this happened."

Larry nodded in agreement.

"Do you think Kathy would come in to see me?"

"I think so. She's just as confused as I am right now."

Kathy was a slender, attractive, brown-haired woman who was one year younger than her husband. She reached for the box of tissues positioned near her chair as soon as she sat down. About a week had passed since Larry told her of his brief affair. She was crushed.

"I always thought Larry was different from all those other men," she cried. "How could he do this to me? I've worked so hard to please him. I've been a good wife to him even though I have a job."

Kathy was understandably angry and hurt. She felt betrayed—seduced and abandoned. But, above all, she wanted to know why it happened.

"There could be many reasons," I said. "And the only way to discover them is to take a good, hard look at yourselves—at your life together and at yourselves as individuals. Both of you have to take some time out of your busy days and begin to question—everything. Why do people do the things they do?"

Kathy shook her head in bewilderment.

"In one respect, you're very lucky," I said. "Larry told you about his affair, voluntarily. He did so because he felt very badly about it. Larry took the first step. He brought it out into the open. It doesn't excuse what he did. But it allows both of you to deal with it. Now is the time to look over the past few months and years in order to identify the factors that contributed to Larry's behavior. You may be able to see patterns that pointed to a breakdown in your marriage. Once you see them, you can begin to change them."

"How can we do all this?"

"The two of you have to be willing to do it, and I'm going to try to help you. We'll talk. I'll meet with both of you together and sometimes separately. But you and Larry will have to do most of the talking yourselves."

"We haven't talked much lately."

"Now's the time to start."

She nodded in agreement.

I explained to Kathy the reasoning behind such counseling. Physically, we are what we are because of our parents. The same is largely true about our emotional makeup—we have derived most of our emotional strengths and weaknesses from our parents. All of us have developed some degree of neuroses. If we expect to go through life without experiencing problems, we are kidding ourselves.

Kathy was a little uneasy about coming to me. After all, it was Larry who had cheated, not she. She grew even more uncomfortable when I talked about the fact that many of our strengths and weaknesses come from our parents. I could sense that she didn't want to think of her parents as being anything but perfect.

This is a critical moment in marriage counseling. If it is to be successful in helping a couple understand and solve their problems, both parties must cooperate fully. Kathy knew that, but she seemed fearful of facing the process of examining her past. She wanted to know how long it would take.

"There's no answer to that," I said. "If you and Larry were going from New York to California, it would be almost impossible to take a direct route. If you drove, you would follow roads that twist and turn to bypass major obstacles. If you took a train, it would stop in every large city along the way. Even if you flew, you would have to skirt around weather patterns, maybe stop off in one or two cities on the way, and circle the airport a few times before landing.

"A psychological journey is similar. To understand what has happened to your marriage, you and Larry are going to have to take a psychological trek back through the early years of your life together—your courtship, your previous romances, your teenage life, your childhood—even back to your birth and conception. That's a long journey. You can't expect to travel it in a direct route. You will have to check your map and move from city to city, perhaps with side trips along the way."

"Yes, but we have problems now. How can we keep living together all this time?"

"Kathy, there is no quick solution. But I think you'll find that if you and Larry start talking about it now, you should begin to see progress soon. You'll get over some of the pain, some of the anger, and some of the resentment. Your marriage didn't get into trouble overnight."

Both Kathy and Larry indicated that they would continue their sessions with me. Both seemed to want to understand their own behavior better.

It was a good sign.

So we began the long journey into the past. The first step was to discover how Kathy and Larry met, what their dating experiences were like, the circumstances surrounding their decision to marry, and, as much as possible, to recreate the day-to-day details of their lives together.

Kathy remembered that Larry had been different from the other boys she knew. He wasn't an animal. She didn't have the problem that her girl friends always talked about—having to fight off overzealous dates. She respected Larry for that. The only thing that bothered her about him was his inability to take care of little details. But she enjoyed doing those things for him.

As for Larry, he really admired the way Kathy watched over her mother. She was so considerate that whenever they were on a date, she took time to call home and check on Mother. Larry knew from the very start that Kathy would made a good wife.

They had met while Larry was in his first year of law school and Kathy was finishing her computer training. It was love at first sight. Soon they announced to their families that they would be married the following summer. Larry's parents were mildly upset at his decision to marry before finishing school. But when they met Kathy, they approved of his choice. She seemed to be a very considerate girl and was a hard worker around the house even when she was a guest.

Kathy's mother, a widow, was worried that the couple might not have enough money to live on. She suggested that they move in with her until Larry finished law school. That would give them a good start. She was delighted when they accepted.

Throughout his remaining years in law school, Larry enjoyed the convenience of coming home to two women who attended to his every need. His own time was free for study. Kathy got a job and still managed to help her mother with the housework and cooking. Larry felt very lucky.

By the time graduation arrived, Mother was a fixture in the family. Neither Kathy nor Larry gave any serious consideration to moving to a home of their own. The early years of law practice would not be lucrative. They knew they would have to work hard to make the money stretch from one paycheck to another. Both felt they were very lucky to have Kathy's mother around.

Sex, for both Kathy and Larry, did not seem to be terribly important. They made love two or three times a week, but it was largely ritual. Kathy admitted to me that she often pretended to reach orgasm. Her genuine orgasms were infrequent.

But soon Larry began to change, so subtly that he didn't realize it at first. He would find himself sneaking off to the bathroom to masturbate to the fantasy of a blonde centerfold he had once seen in a copy of *Playboy* magazine. He loved Kathy, but somehow he couldn't bring himself to talk to her about the sexual practices that he sometimes heard about in court. Sex became a silent tug-of-war with Kathy. Larry wanted his wife to be the blonde bombshell, but he didn't know how to tell her that.

Kathy continued to find sex rather uninteresting. She tried to respond to Larry's advances, but she knew she was holding something back. Larry found more and more of his relief in the bathroom. The guilt feelings began to grow inside him, but he rationalized that the woman in the magazine would merely be his little secret.

The situation dragged on for a time. Larry became a successful lawyer. Though they had money now, the couple continued to live with Kathy's mother. She was growing older and needed to be near her daughter. Then Beth came to work at the law office. She was blonde.

We went farther back into Larry's past.

His father had been a school janitor. From his earliest moments, Larry could remember his father apologizing for the mundane life he led. His own son would "be something," he vowed. So he toiled at his menial job to save up money for Larry's college years. He worked hard to pay his moral dues, too, mowing the lawn at the church, setting up the chairs for bingo, and helping pass the collection plate.

Larry went to church regularly because his father said it was the right thing to do. The Little Leaguers used to tease him as he made his way to serve Mass as an altar boy. Larry recalled wishing he could be out playing baseball while he was in church. He couldn't understand why he had to serve at Mass both Saturday night and Sunday morning.

There were memories of going to the movies with his father. Invariably they would see a crime movie. Father also loved books about crime. He pointed out all the newspaper articles about the Mafia. It was hard for Larry to reconcile his father's interest in both religion and crime. Perhaps, I suggested, his father's extreme interest in church was a way of ridding himself of his guilt over the fantasies of crime.

Larry's mother also wanted her son to be a success. Everything she did was geared to that mission. Larry remembered one event very clearly—the death of his mother's only brother. He told me about the crushing scene of grief in the living room after the funeral, when his grandmother collapsed on the sofa. She kept moaning that her only son was gone. After that, Larry received a lot more attention from his grandmother. She and Mother shepherded him through accordion, swimming, tennis, and sailboat lessons. They would sit proudly on the sidelines and watch him experience life to the fullest. Sometimes he complained about all the lessons. He wanted to know why he couldn't just go out like the rest of the boys and learn on his own.

But both Mother and Grandmother thought he should do things right or not at all.

In his early teens, Larry became aware of a growing interest in girls. But any remark he made about girls or sex was immediately cut off by whoever happened to be around—Grandmother, Mother, or Father. He realized that he had never even seen his mother and father kiss. Mother seemed to recoil whenever Father moved to touch her.

One day Larry was home alone. Curious teenagers often rummage around in their parents' room to find whatever deep, dark, adult secrets might be there. Well, Larry found one. It was a copy of *Playboy* magazine, taped to the bottom of one of his father's dresser drawers. He looked curiously at the beautiful centerfold photograph of the naked blonde girl. So this was Dad's secret! Carefully he replaced the magazine and went into the bathroom to masturbate.

He remembered, too, the family scandal. Uncle Bruce, his father's older brother, went to jail on a numbers charge at the age of sixty-eight! Larry's father was enraged at the shame and scorn his brother had brought upon the respectable family. Then an idea began to form in Larry's mind. He knew how he could please his parents and restore the family's good name. He would become a lawyer.

From that moment on, his family held him in awe. He was not expected to do any work around the house, for he needed time to spend on his studies. During his high school and college days, he did almost nothing else but study. He showed disdain for those students who were irresponsible enough to waste time and money by going out with girls. His sex life was limited to masturbating to the fantasy of the blonde centerfold.

Larry graduated from college with honors. His parents beamed with pride as he marched down the aisle to get his diploma. They threw a big party to celebrate both his graduation and his acceptance by one of the most prestigious law schools in the country. They knew the tuition would be high, but no sacrifice was too great for their son.

Larry's first experience away from home came at the age of twenty-two, when he left to attend law school. He studied hard even though he found small matters getting in his way, such as doing his own laundry, running out for a hamburger, and washing his car. But he worked determinedly and spent his nights at the university's law library. There he met Kathy, who worked part-time as a librarian to help pay her tuition at computer school. She helped Larry quickly hunt up the volumes he needed. She was pretty and had beautiful brown hair, and Larry found himself thinking about her a lot.

One afternoon he lingered at the library to talk to Kathy. Then he excused himself, saying that he was going to McDonald's for a hamburger. Kathy made a face. "Momma is making roast turkey. Why don't you come home with me for dinner?"

Kathy's dominant memory of her childhood had to do with the many happy hours she spent with her father.

"He was such a good man," she recalled. "He played

with me a lot and often took care of me while mother was busy cleaning. He even bathed me until I was five or six years old."

Sometimes Kathy and her father would snuggle together in front of the television while mother put another load of laundry into the washing machine. And if little Kathy woke up during the night, crying from a bad dream, Father would leave his nice warm bed and crawl in with her. "My friends were all jealous of how well I got along with my father," she told me.

When she was eighteen, Kathy's father died suddenly. After her initial anguish, she realized that she would have to become the provider for the family. There was enough insurance money to pay most of her way through technical school. After that, Kathy would have to take care of Mother—at least until she got married to a man who could provide for both of them.

Then she met Larry at the law library. He was so studious and ambitious. She knew right away that he would be successful.

Kathy and Larry now found themselves in a classic psychological dilemma. Both had been raised by overprotective parents who did not allow their children to separate from them properly and become adult individuals in their own right. At the time of their marriage, neither Kathy nor Larry was looking for an adult mate. They were both looking for substitute parents.

Larry was attracted to his future wife because of her mothering attitude toward him. He needed someone to cook for him, to wash his clothes, buy his underwear, and remind him to brush his teeth, so that he could concentrate on the important things in life. When he went to bed with Kathy, he was going to bed—psychologically speaking—with his mother. No wonder he had difficulty being passionate. No wonder he had to take refuge in dreams of a wild blonde sexpot.

Kathy, sheltered and overprotected throughout her childhood, had not been given the self-confidence and courage necessary to face adulthood as a wife. When she found herself without a father, she panicked. She tried to take on the responsibilities of earning money and caring for her mother, but she grabbed the first opportunity to find a man to replace her father. True, Larry had his faults. But so had her father. Mother had always handled all the mundane housekeeping chores for him. Larry's strength was his ability to face the outside world like a man. He would earn a comfortable living and shelter Kathy from life's hardships.

When Kathy went to bed with Larry, she was sleeping—again, psychologically speaking—with her father. So how could she respond sexually? Yet she knew she had to accept sex. She decided simply to lie there and put up with it, not knowing why she didn't like it.

During therapy, both Kathy and Larry began to realize that they had to stop thinking of themselves as children. Little Kathy had been in love with her father, which is normal for all young girls. Her response, also normal, was to copy Mother so that when she grew up she would marry someone just like Father. Perhaps the worst decision Kathy ever made was not to leave home when she graduated from high school and later when she married Larry. No matter what she did, she would always be the little girl in that particular house.

Kathy also began to realize that there had been overtones of incest in her relationship with her father. Whenever she went to bed with Larry, she had pangs of guilt from her childhood memories. Finally she understood why she sometimes jumped back with a shudder when Larry touched her—in effect, she had "married" her father.

Larry had left home physically, but not emotionally. Except for a year in a dormitory, where he did little to care for himself, Larry moved out of his parents' home into Kathy's parents' home. Both Kathy and her mother were so used to pampering men—and Larry was so used to being pampered—that they were happy to have someone to cater to once again. Kathy became more like a mother to Larry than a wife.

Larry also came to realize an interesting point about the color of his wife's hair. It was the same color as his mother's—brown. But the object of Larry's sexual fantasy was a blonde. Why had he chosen a woman who seemed to be the opposite? Larry realized that he had been trained with an unhealthy double standard about sex. His father was very religious and echoed the priest's condemnation of anything sexual. Yet Larry had found the *Playboy* hidden in his father's dresser drawer. The message was confusing—sex was forbidden, yet interesting if kept secret. Larry began to face the fact that his religious training at home and at school came from a very narrow point of view. During therapy, he permitted himself to question those beliefs for the first time.

Then suddenly Larry remembered an incident he had forgotten, or, rather, repressed. (This recollection of buried experiences is a main goal of therapy.) He told me about a time when he had been combing his mother's long, brown, wavy hair. He had experienced a brief sexual feeling and then an intense sense of guilt. How could he be sexually attracted to his own mother?

Could it have been that, as Larry learned to masturbate, he turned to thoughts of the blonde centerfold because a dark-haired girl would have been too close to home? Did Kathy's brown hair help him deny the fantasies that made him feel so guilty?

Slowly Kathy and Larry came to the realization that they had to do at least two things to save their marriage. First, they had to move to a house of their own, where they could belatedly begin their lives as adults. Second, they had to stop reacting to one another as though they were each other's parents—in bed and everywhere else. They needed to view each other as adults with basic sexual needs to fulfill.

They had been married for six years. Now it was time for them to start living together.

Kathy agonized over the decision to leave her mother. She thought of a thousand excuses to stay.

"Kathy," I said, "cross two fingers and hold them tightly together." I often tell my patients to do this. "When you were a tiny fetus in your mother's uterus, you were like that, one with her, even sharing the very same blood. Now uncross your fingers but hold them next to each other as tightly as possible. When you were first born, you looked like that, still attached physically. Then the doctor cut the cord. Now spread your fingers slightly."

She did. She stared at the gap between the fingers.

"That represents the process that should have begun the moment the doctor cut the cord. Now move your two fingers as far apart as possible. That is how you should be as an adult. If your parents, particularly your mother, skillfully severed the emotional umbilical cord, you would become a separate, independent, adult human being. If one of your fingers was accidentally chopped off, the other would continue to function. Even if one or both of your parents died, you would be able to function. Separately. Independently. As an adult."

Kathy left the office that day determined to change. Though it would be painful for her, she and Larry decided to buy their own home and move away from Mother.

Mother went into hysterics. She developed colitis. She was sick for days with headaches. She pouted. Kathy shed many tears in the privacy of her bedroom, but she dried them and went out house-hunting with Larry. They found a home not too far away, but beyond walking distance. After making a down payment, they prepared to move in.

It is part of a person's growth process to separate from his or her parents and become an individual with his or her own identity. The degree of success you achieved in separating from your own parents will have a direct bearing on how successful you are at letting your children separate from you, as well. A parent who cannot let go is a danger to her or his child's health. A doting mother has no right to merge her life so entirely with her child's. Men and women whose parents may be thousands of miles away (or even dead) have not yet accepted their rights to be separate beings. They feel a tremendous sense of guilt for leaving the mother or father, who now suffers so much from loneliness.

That suffering can be either implied or implicit. But either way, the message is clear. "How can you do this to me? You have no right to desert me. You owe me. I gave everything up for you and you have no right to go." Parents communicate intense disappointment and pain. And always there is the invisible burden of guilt placed upon the child.

A woman who finds herself completely satisfied with staying in the house and involves herself in little besides raising children is setting herself up for just such an emotionally uncomfortable situation. The best preventive medicine is to take steps early to establish your own identity—first as a person, then as a mother. Certainly motherhood is important. But it is a limited career. What are you going to do when you retire at forty-five? Unless you develop other outlets for your energy and creativity, you will face boredom at best, loneliness and depression at worst. Try to remember that you will be a *better* parent by neglecting some of the finer points of motherhood in order to develop your own personality more fully. Smothering is not healthy for you, and it can even be worse for your child.

After Kathy and Larry moved to their own home, Kathy's mother began to plague her with phone calls three and four times a day. Kathy summoned up a surprising amount of strength and laid down a rule. One phone call per day—no longer than ten minutes. If Mother called more often, Kathy would hang up. Mother's colitis and headaches continued to plague her, but Kathy remained firm. She was troubled by her mother's strong reaction, but she was happier nonetheless—more relaxed and sure of herself away from her mother's watchful eye.

But Kathy still had some very painful sessions with me. During one, I asked her how she would feel if she learned that her mother had suddenly died. Tears came to her eyes, and she said she would feel hopeless and abandoned. And she would feel terribly guilty for having run out on her. She shook her head to block out the thought.

"I don't want to talk about it," she declared.

I pressed her. "Kathy, what do you feel like when someone you know dies, and you go to the viewing?"

"I don't go to viewings. I hate them."

"Why?"

"I . . . I don't like to think about death."

"But everybody dies. Death is a fact of life." Kathy shuddered. "Your mother *will* die someday," I reminded her. "You can't deny that reality forever."

"What do I do about it?"

"Well, I think you're moving in the right direction. The more you establish your own individual identity, the more you would be able to cope with the death of someone you love. You will be upset, but you'll know that you can make your own way through life."

I pointed out that the current colitis attacks might not be as painful as the guilt her mother might feel later on when she someday has to face the fact that she did not prepare her daughter for adulthood.

In another session, I asked Kathy what would she do

if Larry suddenly ran off with Beth. Again a look of horror crossed her face. "Do we have to talk about this?" she sobbed. "Larry's not going to leave me. I know he isn't. He can't."

"I don't think he will either, but why can't he?"

"He . . . he won't."

"But what if he does?"

Kathy cried into the tissue. She didn't want to answer me.

"Kathy," I said, "I hope that you and Larry have a long, happy life together. And I think you can. But someday—maybe in fifty years, maybe tomorrow—you are going to stop living together. What if Larry was killed in an accident? What would you do?"

"I don't know. I don't know if I could live without him."

"But what about your work? You manage very nicely by yourself on the job. You can't just give up on life."

Kathy looked down at her hands as they twisted in her lap. "I guess I could survive," she agreed. "But I don't know how." She grew silent. I watched as she looked at her fingers, then spread two of them apart. Suddenly she nodded. "I see what you mean. I see what you've been talking about all these months."

"Kathy, no one can take care of you but you."

Larry, too, soon felt better about himself. For the first time in his life, he began to take an active role in caring for his home. Larry bought a few books on home repair, studied them hard, and found that he was not as helpless at mechanical jobs as he had thought. And since Kathy no longer had her mother's help around the house, Larry pitched in with some of the cleaning and cooking. He hated cleaning, but he discovered, to his surprise, that Kathy hated it too! They had a good laugh over that.

Larry discovered that there was satisfaction in something other than his professional career. He stopped working so many evenings and weekends. Once in a while, when he found that he *had* to go into the office on Saturday, he took Kathy with him. Her old job at the law library had made her an expert at hunting up legal precedents. Some Saturdays they would go into the office in the morning, have lunch in a restaurant, and then spend the afternoon shopping for household items. They also talked about going into politics together.

As I had hoped, their sex life improved almost by itself. Larry was more loving, more attentive to the fact that Kathy was a sexual human being rather than a mother figure. Kathy was more adventuresome and sensuous, more interested in Larry as a man. They soon began to experiment with new sexual positions and techniques. Larry found himself able to sustain intercourse over a longer period of time. Kathy found herself responding. By learning more about each other as people—by confiding in each other their thoughts, dreams, and feelings—they learned how to please one another in bed.

Larry and Kathy are no longer receiving therapy. When I last saw them—together for a final session—they seemed well on their way to a happy marriage. They are sharing the tasks of marriage and the joys of living together, away from Kathy's mother. Both have accepted the responsibilities of adulthood, and they are beginning to function as independent human beings. They stand a good chance of never fighting another bout with adultery.

CHAPTER

8

Margaret and John

Margaret and John had been married for thirty-five years. A self-made man, John was the owner of a chain of shoe stores. Margaret had borne three children, the last of whom had recently graduated from college when she first came to see me. Her complaint was sexual frustration, which she blamed on her husband.

She told me that John began having problems when the nation's economy went sour. Caught short of cash, John worried about the future of his business. He found himself unable to sleep well. He would rise at four o'clock in the morning and work on his account books. He grew careless about his appearance. He stayed later and later at the store, trying to keep his faltering business from bankruptcy. In bed with Margaret, he became impotent.

"Could there be another woman?" Margaret asked me, sobbing.

"I just don't know," I said. "John seems to be showing signs of depression. Do you think he will come in to see me?"

"I'll ask him," Margaret said, "but I don't know. He's been so worried about the stores."

John agreed to make an appointment. When I saw him, he looked as if he was fighting a battle inside. He was tense and nervous, and there were deep circles under his eyes. Throughout the session, he chain-smoked constantly.

The first thing I did was take John's blood pressure. Although I felt that the reasons for John's impotence might be emotional problems caused by the economic difficulties he was experiencing, I could not rule out physical causes. The pressure measured 240/130 (anything over 140/80 is high), and I knew that I had to scare him into doing something about it.

I talked to John about the condition. First, the high blood pressure was a physical problem all its own, whether or not it contributed to his impotence. He might also have diabetes. In an advanced case of diabetes, and sometimes very early in the course of the disease, the nerve endings of the blood vessels supplying the penis will be affected. This can result in impotence. I referred him to a urologist and internist who would test for the various possibilities and institute the necessary treatment.

However, John also showed real signs of emotional disease. His nervousness, sleeplessness, and irritability were all indications of psychological depression, which could be causing the impotence. And it was also conceivable—quite likely, in fact—that both physical and emotional problems were besetting him. What he needed, I told him, was treatment for both.

John went to the urologist and internist. Tests for diabetes were negative. He began taking medication for his high blood pressure. He lost weight, and gradually the pressure drifted down. Sleep came a bit easier for him. The economy picked up and business improved.

Once every week or two, he and Margaret would try to make love. But he remained impotent. We were still searching for the cause when in exasperation he told me one day, "But I'm not impotent with Jill!"

Weeks of therapy passed. Even though John now realized that he had to tell Margaret about his affair, he never seemed to be able to find the right moment to talk. During this time, Margaret grew increasingly frustrated because she had learned that her husband's impotence did not seem to be caused by any physical problems. As she left my office one day, still unaware of John's adultery, she vowed that she was going to have it out with him that night.

Several days later she came in for an emergency appointment. She had not slept more than a few hours in the three nights since John had finally admitted his affair to her. Margaret's face was haggard and drawn, and her hair was a mess. "I gave him the best years of my life!" she screamed. "How could he do this to me?" Margaret wanted to kick John out of the house. She wanted an immediate divorce. She wanted to shoot both John and his mistress.

As a woman, I could understand her feelings. As a psychiatrist, I tried gently to quiet her down, to get her to wait a few weeks before making any decisions about the future. Margaret said she would think it over. But her feelings of anxiety and depression were so great that I prescribed medication to relieve her suffering until she could gain control over herself once again.

After a couple of weeks had passed, Margaret was calm enough to begin to act more rationally. My task now was to get her to see the importance of understanding John's behavior. Only then could the two of them make a knowledgeable decision about the future of their marriage.

"In a sense, your husband may have been a victim of pressures he could not control," I said.

"What do you mean?"

"Emotional problems are just as real as physical ones. If John suffered from headaches, you wouldn't berate him for them. You would understand that a headache can be a symptom of various physical conditions, such as poor eyesight, high blood pressure, or even a brain tumor. Adultery is not a disease any more than a headache is. It is a symptom. It is a sure sign that something has gone wrong . . ."

"In John," Margaret said.

"In your marriage," I corrected. "What has happened indicates that something is preventing the two of you from maintaining a loving relationship with one another."

"So he has problems. We all have problems. That doesn't excuse him," Margaret snapped.

"No, it doesn't excuse him. But it can help you understand what he has been going through."

Margaret grew thoughtful. Then she said, "Okay. So what do we do?"

"If John had headaches, he might go to the family doctor, right? Any competent physician would ask him a whole range of questions that might seem unrelated to headaches. He would ask about shortness of breath, weakness, nosebleeds, dizzy spells, or tingling feelings. He is looking for clues to the cause of the headaches and he is taking the opportunity to give John a general checkup as well.

"We're going to do the same thing with your emotional systems—yours and John's. The mind is made up of memories, attitudes, inhibitions, judgments, and feelings—all of which are constantly brought to bear upon the major functional areas of your life, such as your marriage. We've got to explore how well all these systems are working for you and John in order to be able to understand the symptom—the affair."

"I'll try," Margaret said, a slight tremor in her voice betraying some reservations.

When John was two years old, his father had a mild heart attack. From that point on, life changed dramatically for the man. He was laid up at home for extended periods of time, which left the family finances in a precarious situation. Father spent most of his days and evenings stretched out on the sofa, for he was plagued with a mysterious weakness that baffled the doctors. According to them, the heart attack had not been severe enough to cause this weakness. Nevertheless, John's father complained about it constantly. The subject dominated the few family conversations.

Mother was left with the task of raising, disciplining, entertaining, and educating Johnny. With a husband who could die at any moment—as he frequently reminded her—she needed someone to lean on. And she chose to lean on Johnny. It was almost as though she was married to the boy. He followed her around the house, helping out with chores, carrying on adultlike conversations with her.

When Johnny was four, Mother became pregnant again. Years later he questioned how she could have become pregnant when Father was always so weak and sickly, and he wondered if perhaps Father didn't question it also. His sister Sally was born just before Johnny's first day of school.

"I can remember the scene vividly even today," he told me. "I got all dressed up in my Sunday clothes. I said good-bye to Dad, who was on the sofa. Then I walked out the door. I turned to wave to Momma. She was standing in the doorway holding the baby. When the school bus came, I looked up at all the kids' faces peering out the windows at me. I stopped dead in my tracks. This dizzy feeling came all over me, and I turned and ran back to Momma."

John remembered his mother trying all sorts of strategies to get him to go to school. It was months before he trotted off to school without throwing a fit. And for years, he went out the door with a scowl on his face.

Life changed even more dramatically when Johnny was eight. Father died of the heart attack he had so long predicted. Little Johnny became "the man of the house." Every day after school, he rushed home to mow the lawn, paint the shutters, and help Momma out in any way he could. He never did like school, so he quit as soon as he was sixteen and found a job as a clerk in a shoe store. He was a good, willing worker, and he moved up fast in the job. Before long, he was assistant manager and had dreams of someday opening his own store.

John was never attracted to girls his own age. From time to time, he met older women, and he experienced a series of shallow sexual relationships with them. But he never really got involved. When he was between girl friends, he would sometimes go to see a prostitute. He liked that because he could get sexual relief quickly and without emotional complications.

One summer the manager of the store hired a college girl to help out. She was a couple of years older than John. From the moment he saw her, he thought she was beautiful.

Margaret was the eldest of ten children. One of her earliest memories was of an incident that took place when she was about four years old. Someone came from the board of health, and she remembered her mother and father being very upset and fighting after the visit. Mother ran out and was gone for days. Father busied himself by cleaning up the filth in the house. Margaret could still smell the strong disinfectant he used. The inspector from the board of health returned a few days later and seemed satisfied. But Margaret remembered him saying that if they found the house in such a mess again, they would have to remove the children.

Mother came home a few days later, smirking and almost daring Father to ask her where she'd been. She slipped back into the same old pattern of spending most of the day on the telephone with her girl friends. The house became a shambles once again.

Margaret, as the oldest, did her best to help her father keep the house clean. She was always afraid the inspector would return and remove the children. Since Mother was usually off somewhere with her girl friends, Margaret and Father developed a close relationship. The two of them knew they were responsible for keeping the family together.

Margaret was known as a child mature for her age. A good student, she was always ready to help with chores in her classroom. At recess, she preferred to stand near the teacher and carry on a conversation instead of joining the other kids in games. She matured fast physically, too. Her figure began to take shape when she was ten. Mother, who was very thin, suggested that Margaret might want to bind her chest to make it flatter like the rest of the girls. Margaret became embarrassed about her body, but there was little she could do to hide it.

Because of her excellent grades, Margaret won a scholarship to college. Her father was pleased and proud because he didn't have enough money to pay for her tuition. So at the age of eighteen, Margaret went off to school. The scholarship paid her expenses during the academic year, but in the summertime, she needed to work to make money. She found a job in a shoe store.

John was immediately impressed by the meticulous manner in which Margaret approached her job. She breezed into the store and quickly persuaded the manager to let her rearrange the stock. Her new system was a great improvement. John found himself watching her ample chest move up and down as she busied herself in the stockroom.

Margaret thought highly of the handsome young man who already was assistant manager. They were soon eating lunch together every day. She eagerly participated in John's dreams of someday owning a chain of prosperous shoe stores. In her own mind, she began to picture herself as the wife who helped this respected businessman manage his stores. They would be accepted into the highest social circles.

Of course, Margaret realized that John would have to change. He dressed rather sloppily, and he needed to pay more attention to his manner with people. Professionally, he had to gain more experience with knowing just the right kind of merchandise to order. But these things were no problem. She could guide him once they were married.

Summer ended, and Margaret went back to college. She came home frequently on weekends to see John. John was a perfect gentleman, and they always had a good time together.

John admitted to me that he had longed to explore Margaret's chest, but he didn't want to upset her. She was a respectable woman. So he still found his sexual outlet in brief affairs with casual acquaintances.

Margaret respected John's polite attitude toward her body. But as their love grew, and as she matured, she grew restless. She wished that he would make an advance. Finally one weekend she came home from college determined that she was going to lose her virginity. Late Saturday night, in the backseat of John's car, Margaret made her intentions clear. Their sex was fast and furious. Margaret wondered why everyone seemed to make such a big fuss over it. Nevertheless, she went back to college with a satisfied smile on her face.

They dated for two more years and finally got married the weekend after Margaret graduated from college. They settled into life. John opened his own shoe store, then another. Before long, he had a successful chain. Margaret helped out at first, but then she became pregnant and took care of her duties at home.

Margaret and John were from the "old school." Sex was not supposed to be so important. So if neither of them really enjoyed it—well, they would just live with that. For years, the two of them were content with a less-than-ideal marriage.

They settled into a routine of taking care of business. John managed the shoe stores. Margaret raised the kids. Occasionally there were vague stirrings of discontent with the marriage. John chafed at Margaret's obsession with cleanliness. How he longed for the chance to take his children and wallow in a mud hole for a while! Margaret bitched about John's sloppiness. She was sure that she could do wonders to clean up the operation of the shoe stores, but John kept that activity all to himself. Margaret felt isolated at home. Her solution was to work extrahard at raising the children properly.

For many women like Margaret, children provide the only reason for being. Since children are all they have, they cling to motherhood tenaciously, and in so doing, neglect their role as wives. They forget to be good companions for their husbands both in and out of bed, and so these husbands and wives grow further and further apart. What's more, these supermothers are unconcerned—and often even unaware—that their husbands might like to participate more in the great adventure of raising children. This can and should be one of the experiences that binds a man and a woman closely together.

For the most part, John and Margaret lived their lives quietly and without incident. Then a gradual change began to take place as, one by one, the three children grew up and left home. Margaret, stuck in the house with time on her hands, began to read and hear a lot more about female sexual enjoyment. At first, she scoffed at the idea, but then she began to pay more attention to it. Could she, in her fifties, finally learn to get enjoyment out of sex? Very cautiously she began to approach the subject with John.

John found himself strangely uneasy. In the back of his mind, he was worried about many things. Was he destined to die before his time with a heart ailment? He took stock of his life. Somehow success seemed flat. He was proud of his business, but he couldn't seem to view shoe stores as any great social service. The economy had gone sour. Now even his businesses were threatened. The first thing people stopped buying when money was tight was shoes. John didn't know where to turn. He couldn't sleep at night. He took refuge in food. He deliberately paid less attention to his appearance, knowing it would goad Margaret. And he found himself paying a lot of attention to his bookkeeper, an attractive woman in her forties. Maybe an affair was what he needed, he thought. Life was short. He had to do something exciting before it passed him by completely.

And so he found a lover. He found the sex to be more

exciting than his relations with Margaret. But he found it extremely difficult to deal with his guilt feelings. He was a despicable person, he thought, for doing this to his loving wife. Sex with Margaret, never really enjoyable, now became impossible.

We must all be wary of waking up some fateful morning in our late forties or early fifties wondering whether it is worth getting out of bed. What is our purpose for being? Our children don't need us, our careers are set, we are at the top of the pay scale, sex is boring, and there isn't enough money to travel (and one city looks like the next, anyway). We feel too old to start anything new. We wonder how much time is left as we face the downhill side of life. In order to cope with this mid-life crisis, we must take positive action. This is the time for husband and wife to search together for new goals, for finding new meaning and purpose in life. Together, they should look at their relationship (and their lives) and examine where they are going, what's happening with both, and where they are and where they think they would like to go. (It is a good idea for a couple to do this every five years or so, but it is never too late to start this process of evaluation.) This is no easy task and could be the subject for an entire book.

Instead of bringing these feelings into the open with Margaret, John hid them. They remained inside, tearing at him until they burst into the open. He suddenly saw Jill as his ticket to a new life. It didn't matter that Jill was married and had her own set of problems—her own reasons for wanting an affair—John saw her as the answer.

"Do you love Jill?" I asked him.

"I don't know."

"Do you still love Margaret?"

"I'm not sure."

There would be no easy answers for John and Margaret. A lot of long, hard work lay ahead. John knew that he could no longer juggle two women. He had to choose one or the other. And I was not at all sure if Margaret could hold up under the strain of the tension between them. She was also having difficulty dealing with her own feelings of failure—failure to change John into the neat husband she had always envisioned, failure to become involved in the family business, failure to provide John with an enjoyable sex life, failure to achieve a perfect marriage. Beneath all this was a growing anxiety about aging and being left alone if John should die suddenly. Now that the children were gone, John was all she had.

I persuaded them both to continue to see me on a regular basis. Margaret made some early progress in therapy. She began to see how her own mother's sloppiness and irresponsibility had contributed to her current passion for neatness and her intolerance toward any show of laziness. She even began to acknowledge that she probably overdid things once in a while. Margaret saw that she had relied too heavily upon her children's need for her, and that now she had a void in her life that needed to be filled. She had to become a wife and helpmate once more. She persuaded John to let her redecorate one of the stores. But every advance in her therapy seemed to come grudgingly. Margaret was such a perfectionist that she had difficulty admitting her own shortcomings.

I tried to find out how much Margaret actually knew about her husband. I found that she did not understand his business, nor did she seem to care about it as long as he paid the bills. She knew little about his feelings or his hopes and fears for the future. This indicated either that John had kept himself hidden from her, or that Margaret had not tried hard enough to learn to know him.

"I keep telling him that we have to sit down and talk," Margaret assured me.

"When do you expect to do this?" I asked.

"As soon as he comes home from work, he sticks his nose inside the newspaper. And I have so many things I want to talk to him about."

"Maybe that's not the time to talk to him."

"Well, I've been sitting around all day, waiting for him to come home!"

"Yes, but he's been waiting all day to get home and relax, to change pace. When he first comes home, he's not in the mood for a heavy discussion. You need to recognize this and try to decide when might be the best time to talk with him."

Margaret acknowledged the point. "I know it's not when he first walks in the door."

Margaret had been guaranteeing her own failure. Because of John's affair, she was sure that he would reject her again. And so she chose exactly the wrong time for discussion. She provoked him. She was afraid that he would get mad at her for no reason at all, so she gave him a reason. That way, she thought, it would be easier to accept his rejection.

But John was also making some progress in therapy during this time. He began to see that his impotence was caused by a variety of factors. There would be no magical cure; he would have to deal with all the problems he was facing. His high blood pressure didn't help. But he also, for the first time in his life, voiced anger at his spouse's lack of response in bed. He knew he wasn't pleasing her, and therefore he felt incompetent as a lover. John discussed this problem with Margaret. He also told her about the other things that were troubling him—his fear of a heart attack and of bankruptcy.

Once the two began to talk together about what they really felt, things began to change for the better. Their sex lives, while not ideal, improved. For a time, I thought everything was going to be all right.

Then John seemed to sink into a depression. He fought a battle with Margaret's sleeping pills. Try as he might, he couldn't seem to get Jill out of his mind.

One night John and Margaret tried to make love. He just couldn't seem to find the right position or type of movement that would please her. In frustration, he rolled over.

Margaret looked at him and said, "I bet you know what Jill likes!"

John quickly dressed, packed his bags, and left. He moved in with Jill.

Margaret missed John immediately and wanted him back. She told me she would try harder if only he would return home. She would talk to him more about their sex problems, and she would carefully avoid the subject of the other woman. She would try to show John what techniques she liked in bed—if only he would come back.

"What if he doesn't come back?" I asked. "You have to be strong enough to face any eventuality. We can both hope that John will return so that you can pick up the pieces of your marriage. But you have to be ready to face life on your own if need be."

"But John is all I've got."

"Are you sure? You seem pretty capable of taking care of yourself."

"I can't do anything. I haven't worked in years."

"What about that college degree you worked so hard for? Certainly that shows you are capable."

"Well . . ."

"Sure, you would be happier if John came back and you both found that you could make your love grow. But do you feel worthy of his love? Do you feel capable of giving him the love he wants?"

"I don't know."

"Margaret, I think you've got to do some work on your own personality—whether or not John comes home. You've got to become your own person."

"I've been thinking about getting a job."

"That might be a good start. Then you wouldn't be moping around the house all day. And you'll be able to see that you *can* bring in some money. You *can* take care of yourself."

Margaret got a job in a bookstore. She had always liked to read, and she kept up with the latest best-sellers. Her knowledge of the market and her talent for setting up sales displays quickly helped her get ahead. Before long, she was a buyer for the store.

While she continued to miss John, she began to feel better about herself and her life. Her fear of abandonment subsided. Her children often invited her along on weekend outings. She renewed her driver's license and bought a used car so that she would not be confined to her home.

"The nights are the hardest," she said to me. "It's so quiet and lonely. But you know—part of that is okay. It gives me a chance to think things over. I've got a lot of thinking to do."

John never returned to therapy. I have no idea whether his impotence bothered him anymore.

A year after he moved out, Margaret divorced him. She is not happy about what happened. But she knows now that she is strong enough to live life on her own.

CHAPTER
9

Liz and David

Liz was referred to me by her family doctor. She was extremely attractive and looked like a high-fashion model. Long, jet-black hair hung down below her shoulders. Big, golden loops dangled from her pierced ears. She sat stiffly in the chair across from me.

"I get sick to my stomach all the time," she informed me. "Dizzy, too. The doctor can't find anything wrong with me."

Liz's family doctor had just given her a complete physical examination. He told her that his findings and her medical history revealed a healthy woman of thirty-five years. There seemed to be no physical problem that could be the cause of her symptoms.

I now began to review Liz's emotional systems. We

searched for difficulties in her home; with her children, parents, friends; and in her marriage. Nothing immediately waved a red flag, so I tried to probe deeper, sensing that she was hiding something. One of the questions I asked was, "Do you think your husband has ever cheated on you?"

Liz broke into tears. "David travels a lot. He meets exciting women. I can almost tell when he comes back from a trip whether or not he's fooled around. He's different, sometimes—ashamed of something, I think."

"Have you talked about your fears?" She shook her head. "When he comes home and you suspect him of cheating, is that when you feel sick?"

Liz thought back. To her amazement, she realized that her attacks of nausea and dizziness seemed to occur after David had returned from a trip. Recently, they also occurred when she merely anticipated his leaving. Our first session ended with the agreement that we would continue to explore the psychological reasons for her physical symptoms.

After several sessions, Liz was convinced that at least some of her symptoms were due to her fears about David's behavior. Together we came to the conclusion that the symptoms might subside if she brought the problem out into the open—if she confronted David with her suspicion. A few weeks passed before Liz could gather her courage for the confrontation. Twice she tried to start the critical discussion and then lost her courage, yet even these abortive attempts alerted David to the fact that she knew what was going on. Finally she managed to explain to David that she felt her strange illness was the result of her suspicion about him having an extramarital relation.

David, expecting the "showdown," admitted that he occasionally had sex with another woman when he was out of town. He had been doing so about two or three times a year for several years. But he said he loved Liz. He didn't want to lose her. Somehow he just found himself unable to turn down a night with an attractive woman he met at a convention or board meeting.

Over the next few days, Liz suffered badly. But then her pain began to subside. She was not entirely free from her illness, but she was making progress. She had a long talk with David. Under the threat of divorce, he agreed to come in to see me.

He was thirty-eight and showed no beginnings of a middle-aged paunch. His hair was graying only slightly at the temples. He was a dapper, handsome businessman who had worked his way up the corporate ladder to become comptroller of a large national company.

David was not pleased to be in my office. He answered my questions reluctantly.

"You seem to be nervous," I said.

"I . . . uh . . . never thought I'd have to do this."

"Do what?"

"See a shrink."

"It makes you uncomfortable?"

"Yes."

"Because you don't think you need to be here?"

David remained silent.

"Did Liz force you to come here?"

"Yeah."

"How?"

"She said she'd divorce me if I didn't come."

"Oh. Did she tie you up and drag you here?"

"No."

"Then it sounds to me that at least a part of you wanted to come. There's a part of you that doesn't want a divorce. It would have been very easy not to come if you were willing to get a divorce."

David shrugged again. "Yeah, I guess so." He was quiet for a moment. Then he said, "This sort of thing doesn't come easy for me."

"What sort of thing?"

"Talking about . . . things."

"Things like marriage, love, and other women?" I suggested.

He nodded.

"Why don't we try?"

"Okay."

David's decision to continue to see me was a sign that he was sincere in trying to understand his behavior. But progress was slow. He suffered from a classic fault of the American male—the inability to express his feelings. This is very nearly an epidemic in Western culture. A little boy is taught to act like a man. Whenever he faces an emotional crisis, he is reminded that big boys don't cry. Unlike his sister, who is allowed—even expected—to show wide swings of emotion, he is trained to control himself. He must grow up to face the challenges of life in the cold, hard world. Often the weight of this responsibility produces a businesslike man who not only has few real friends but who is often a stranger to himself.

David was proud of his business successes and largely unaware of his other human feelings. He told me that he felt thick-skinned. He knew he wasn't as sentimental or emotional, as Liz was. That was just a difference between them, he said, and Liz would have to accept it.

But David wasn't being honest with himself. We all have deep feelings. That is part of being human. David suppressed them, but they surfaced in his mannerisms. He was a chain-smoker, a fidgeter, and a worrier over insignificant details. All these things pointed toward emotional problems.

In my view of human behavior, David's occasional episodes of cheating were further manifestations of his suppressed feelings. David disagreed, preferring to treat his extramarital affairs as casual flings that meant nothing to him.

"I love Liz," he said to me one day. "But there are times when, frankly, she gets a little boring. She's a homebody. She has very little connection with what's really going on in the world, except for the world of cosmetics. She spends hours in front of that damn mirror! Sometimes when I meet a woman who's involved with business, with travel, with *my* world, I find her very exciting. Sex is a way of cementing a good friendship. Maybe as a woman you can't understand that. Maybe Liz can't either. But I don't see anything wrong with it. I don't see why it has to make Liz sick or why it has to threaten our marriage. It's just the way it is. I don't think it's possible for me to be 100 percent faithful."

I admitted to David that his view of sex and marriage was one that seemed to be increasingly popular. There are even some psychiatrists who expound the virtues of open marriages, in which a certain amount of extramarital sex is condoned. I asked David if his philosophy worked both ways. How would he react if Liz cheated?

"I'd kill her," he said calmly.

"Double standard?" I suggested.

He shrugged.

Just about everyone feels the need to be close to one other person. Often when a marriage is headed for divorce, one or both partners find a substitute to replace the spouse and fulfill that need for closeness. This, however, was not the case with David. His only close friendship, though far from perfect, was with Liz. His sexual adventures never resulted in any lasting relationships.

I suggested to David that there was something lacking in all this, that a feeling of loneliness seemed to filter through his stories of his casual affairs. He himself had said that one reason for sex was to cement a friendship. He wanted friends. Why, then, did the friendships not seem to last?

David said he didn't know.

Perhaps the sex was actually interfering with potential friendships, I suggested. David, like so many other men, found it difficult to relate to a woman without bringing in a confusing array of sexual undercurrents. Then, once the sex became a reality, David would find that his own guilt feelings (which he tried hard to cover up) made it impossible to continue the friendship.

David was skeptical. He preferred his own philosophy that occasional, casual sex with other women was the natural state of man. But he was aware now that he had to come to terms with how that philosophy affected Liz. I felt that it was important for David to examine his early life experiences to understand the basis for his unsuccessful relationships with women. I planned to begin that journey into the past on the day that David called to cancel his appointment.

Liz cried and clutched at her stomach. "He said he wasn't coming to see you anymore," she sobbed. "He said there's nothing wrong with him and he doesn't need a shr—a woman doctor telling him how to run his life. He said he loved me and he wanted to stay married to me, but I would just have to accept how it is with a man. He said he would try to be faithful, but that he couldn't make any promises. He said it was time for me to grow up and face the facts of life."

"How does that make you feel?"

"It makes me sick."

I felt that David needed help, but I couldn't force him to seek it. Even a therapeutic relationship was impossible for him at the time. So I was now left to work only with Liz. She told me there were two things she wanted. The first was to save her marriage, even if it meant accepting David's view of marriage and fidelity. The thought of divorce was too devastating for her. She couldn't face the prospect of financial worries, the task of raising her children as a single parent, the humiliation, or the loneliness. But Liz also wanted an end to her nausea and dizziness. The symptoms had subsided as long as David was seeing me. When he ran away from therapy, her mysterious illness returned immediately. We continued to explore the psychological causes.

Liz remembered that her mother had always been sickly. Most days she moped around in her bathrobe, complaining of assorted aches and pains, and downing a variety of pills and patent medicines. Her favorite book was a medical dictionary. She would leave it conspicuously opened to pages where she had circled some exotic disease that seemed to match whatever symptoms she was complaining about at the moment.

Her father worked two jobs in order to pay the doctor bills. Liz rarely saw him during the week. He left for his first job early in the morning and returned from the second late at night. On weekends, he slept late in the morning and spent the remainder of the day "relaxing."

It seemed as though Liz's parents had devised a long-standing game they could play with one another. Her mother was a classic hypochondriac, obviously using her complaints to gain attention and sympathy. Her father used the excuse of doctor bills to escape the need to relate to his family. This only made Mother more lonely and more sickly. It was a circle of emotional deficiencies that continued for years.

Liz remembered her senior year in high school as a time of special torture for her mother. One afternoon when Liz returned from school, Mother was doubled over on the sofa, her hands around her stomach. Liz asked what was wrong. Tearfully her mother announced that she could hide the secret no longer. She was facing the onset of menopause, and she feared that the suffering was going to be hell.

And it was. Mother complained of being unable to sleep for fear that she would waken during the night with one of her "terrible sweats." The dizziness she occasionally felt kept her confined to her bed all day long. She didn't dare go shopping because she was scared that she would pass out. Someone had to be with her constantly. Liz's mother was convinced that she would never make it through menopause without somehow developing cancer.

Over a period of many sessions, Liz became aware that her mother wasn't the only one who had suffered from the absence of the man of the house. With tears in her voice, she recalled her sadness every time she looked through the window at her father's back as he got into his car. After he drove away she would go to her mirror and ask, "What's wrong with me? Why does he keep going away?" Then she would start to play with her mother's discarded make-up, trying to make herself "prettier for Daddy." But she never felt pretty enough.

One day she saw her father get into a different car, driven by a woman. This time Liz swayed, grew sick to her stomach, and collapsed on her bed. *How could he?* she wondered. But she was so upset by what she saw that she pretended it didn't happen. She got up and went to complain to her mother about her illness, never again consciously remembering the incident until she came for therapy.

Now her recollection of the event led to important self-discoveries. She realized that not only was she still fearful of being abandoned when David went on trips, but that it was the suppressed memory of her father's apparent infidelity—with all of its physical pain—that was overwhelming her each time. Her conscious mind wouldn't allow her to accept the reality of her father's cheating, so it caused her to focus on her physical symptoms.

Liz also discovered that she was "using" her physical pain because, like her mother, she was afraid of being left alone in her later years. This seemed to be one of the reasons that she couldn't bear to think about divorce. When she suspected David of cheating, she became desperate to hold onto her marriage. So she reacted in the manner that she had been taught all her life. She got sick. Surely her physical suffering would bring her more attention and sympathy from her husband. (It seemed to be working for her mother after forty-three years of marriage.)

Liz was truly convinced that her mother's many illnesses had been serious. But when I pointed out that her mother, at age sixty-four and well over menopause, was still alive and robust (though never without a variety of complaints), I began to see the first doubts enter Liz's mind. Gradually she came to understand the nature of her own symptoms, but it was a long time before her pain began to lessen.

I felt that Liz would continue to suffer until she made some basic decisions. She had to determine how badly she wanted to remain married to David, who was growing more like her father every day. David was hardly ever home, and when he was, he was unable to show affection and express his feelings. Liz remembered that when he had agreed to marry her she had been thrilled to "win out" over all his other girl friends, even those he had during their engagement. She believed that all she had to do to keep him from leaving was to look pretty and stay home, as her mother had done. But David, like Liz's father, was insensitive to his wife's needs. And the feeling that he was her total source of happiness pushed him further away from her.

Since it appeared that David would not stop cheating and neither he nor Liz desired a divorce, I knew the couple would have to come to terms with a marital compromise—an arrangement. Instead of playing childish games with one another—instead of all the lying, hiding, and unexpressed rage—they needed to bring a discussion of David's infidelity out into the open. They needed to set rules. Both of them needed to compromise their positions in order to come up with a type of marriage that each could live with, even though neither would be entirely happy.

Liz gathered her courage to discuss such a compromise with David. She found him surprisingly receptive to the idea. He had become quite worried about Liz's illness and wanted to help. Their talk was tearful and often hostile. But they did manage to hammer out some ground rules. First, David was to be allowed an occasional casual affair. He agreed to try to limit these experiences as much as he could. Further, he agreed that he would have sex with another woman only when that woman knew he was married and knew that the sex would not result in a lasting relationship.

Most important to Liz, David agreed to try to tell her about the affairs, briefly, when they occurred. He knew it was going to be difficult for him. But he also realized that his secrets were building a great wall between himself and Liz. Liz knew that she would be shattered every time David told her, but that she at least could learn the truth.

This is not the sort of marriage that I recommend. In most instances, I would prefer to see a husband and wife rekindle their love for one another—or divorce. But there are times when I have to face the fact that not every patient is able to work toward one of these two alternatives. Sometimes an arrangement is the only method that will help both partners live with their particular emotional problems. But an arrangement will work only when both parties understand what they are gaining and what they are giving up. Liz was willing to accept David's cheating in return for his honesty and security. David had to learn to be open with his feelings, and in return, he would be allowed to cheat on occasion.

There is always considerable doubt about the viability of an arrangement. Talking about it is one thing. But sooner or later, both husband and wife come to grips with the reality of their arrangement. From week to week, I searched for evidence in Liz that would tell me how well she was holding up.

David went on several business trips and came back to report that he had behaved himself. Liz found, eventually, that she could believe him. There was a calmness about David that she could trust. After these trips, she felt no return of her symptoms.

Then came the inevitable time that David exercised his new marital freedom. Liz knew as soon as David walked in the door. And immediately she felt queasy. She collapsed into a chair and struggled to catch her breath. But she composed herself after a few minutes, and they talked late into the night. It was difficult for David to tell his story, because he didn't want to make Liz suffer. But somehow, both of them felt better that there were no secrets.

And Liz discovered that she trusted David's word more and more when he had remained faithful. The trade-off seemed to be working. Liz reduced the frequency of her visits and then stopped coming altogether. When she left my office the last time, she was —if not happy—free from her physical symptoms. She was facing reality.

About a year and a half later, my answering service relayed a message that David had called. I returned the call immediately. He wanted to come in for an appointment.

If anything, David was more nervous than I remembered. I asked him how things were with Liz. How was their compromise working?

"Fine," he said, "for Liz."

"What do you mean?"

"It's very hard for me to say this. I think you were right."

"About what?"

"About my feeling so guilty about all of this. Now that Liz knows about my affairs, I'm torn apart inside when I have to tell her. I don't even have to tell her in words. She can read my face now when I walk in the door."

I remained silent, waiting for him to continue.

"I've tried to stop," he said. "I realized that things would be better if I were faithful to Liz. Sometimes I've stopped for a long time. But then I'll be on a trip, and I'll meet some woman, and. . . . I can't even enjoy the sex now because I know how it will hurt Liz. But I can't seem to quit, either."

Then David shed the first tear I'd ever seen from him. "I'm ready to talk now," he said. "I want to find out why I'm this way."

That happened just recently. David has returned for several sessions, and we are only beginning to look at his life to try to understand and resolve his conflict—his habit of giving a sexual cast to every relationship with a woman. Already I can tell that he probably will not run away again. He is different, willing to cooperate, willing to learn. Whether he can strengthen his personality, whether he can build a stronger, more traditional marriage with Liz, no one knows.

But he is working hard at it now.

PART III

RESOLUTION

CHAPTER

10

Separation

When I first learned of my husband's cheating, my gut reaction was to throw him out. Would that really help?

There are reasons to separate, and there are reasons not to. When you first learn of your husband's infidelity, you generally respond emotionally and do not consider all the consequences. Only when you have had the chance to sit back and think about the reasons for the adultery will you have an opportunity to make a calm decision about the immediate future of your marriage. Let's look at the pros and cons.

The disadvantages of separation. Most important, separation is a form of running away. The situation you are running from may be rotten, but you are fleeing, nevertheless. Even if the differences with your husband are irreconcilable, you must guard against the danger of running too soon. You must be convinced that you have done your very best to save the marriage, or you may suffer from terrible guilt later on.

There is a danger that you or your husband will go straight back to Momma, either physically or emotionally. Mature parents can be a great help during this trying time, but you must consider the fact that your relationship with your parents might be one of the factors that contributed to the adulterous situation in the first place. If this is the case, running to them is only going to make matters worse. You probably already enjoy some of the emotional strengths your parents have, so they cannot help you further. During the crisis, your parents may only be able to reinforce your emotional weaknesses, since without knowing it, they are so frequently the source of them. Parents have difficulty viewing the situation objectively and often take one side or the other completely.

Separation may bring you face to face with a whole range of problems that you are not ready to handle. Who is going to put up the storm windows? How are you going to explain to the department store that you can't pay the charge-card bill? Are you ready to recount the reasons for your separation to the friends, neighbors, and relatives who will surely ask? During this critical time for your marriage, you need to be able to work (with or without your husband) to discover the reasons for the adultery. You need to begin to know and understand yourself and your husband better. It will be difficult to concentrate on these important human questions when you are beset by the wide range of day-to-day problems that come with separation.

The advantages of separation. Separation can also be a positive experience for both husband and wife. It may bring them closer together, or it may become a healthy means of breaking up a terminally ill marriage. Separation disrupts the status quo of your life. Though you are busy with many other considerations, the long, quiet evenings alone will force you to take stock of your marriage and your life. All of us need a certain amount of private time when we can be alone with our thoughts. Separation may provide you with that opportunity for the first time in years.

There may be a divorce in your future. You must face that possibility. Separation will allow you to try it on for size. You may learn that you are capable of accomplishing much more than you thought possible. If the lawn needs mowing, you can do it yourself or arrange for someone else to take care of it. If you haven't been working, you should be able to find a job. As you handle your problems, you will become a more independent, resourceful, complete human being.

In other words, separation from your husband may be an opportunity for you to complete the task of becoming your own person. It may be your own personal Declaration of Independence.

You should weigh all these pros and cons carefully to determine what is the best course of action for you. Obviously such a decision should not be made on the spur of the moment.

My husband told me he wants to leave. Should I try to stop him?

Your husband's life is all mixed up now, complicated beyond his understanding, and probably far different from his youthful fantasies. He must be given a chance to sort out his priorities. Many men find they want neutral ground at this time. They need to get away from wife, children, and home.

I recommend that you let him go. The more you resist, the more he will want to go. His leaving will be very painful. But it is more productive than pressuring him to stay against his will.

Should I let him go even if he wants to live with the other woman?

Yes. He'll want her more if you hold him back.

Will my husband ever come back to me?

The chances are reasonably good that he will. At the moment, he is in love with a fantasy. Perhaps the other woman spends hours preparing for his arrival and is always at her best for him. If he moves in with her, he will suddenly see her in curlers and jeans. He will snuggle up next to the woman's own set of emotional problems. He will realize anew that no relationship is a beautiful fantasy twenty-four hours a day.

There is a more positive reason for letting him go. You have been living together for years. The relationship has grown stale. You take each other for granted. Suddenly alone, your husband may come to realize that now you are the most important thing in the world to him. Separation may provide you with the opportunity for a new beginning.

But what am I going to do about money if my husband leaves?

Since the average American household tries to live on about 120 percent of its income, money is going to be very tight. You and your husband will be supporting two households on just about the same amount of money as before. Rule number one is: *Do not gouge him for money.* First of all, if you are interested in having him back, pressuring him for money will only alienate him further. Second, if you are an able-bodied adult, you are responsible for your own food, clothing, and shelter. If you already work, work harder. If you don't, get a job! This advice may be contrary to what many lawyers will tell you. Some say that the woman should not go to work because it will cut her chances for alimony. I believe that large alimony payments only continue your dependence on your husband. It is far better to earn money for yourself than to sit at home getting more lonely and depressed by the moment.

I don't think I can earn enough money to pay for everything. Does my husband have to help pay the cost of raising the children?

Child-support payments are different from alimony. As the children's father, your husband is just as responsible for their care as you are. But you have an obligation at this time not to squander the money and not to expect of him more than he can give. Spend the money on the children, not on yourself. This will be an unmistakable sign of maturity that will prove that you are acting rationally and compassionately, while the other woman may be pressuring him for a trip to the islands. You will just have to close your eyes and forget about the money he may be spending on *her*.

How should I handle visitation rights?

Visitation rights are often the most disturbing problem for separated parents. Children are caught in the middle. They don't want to break away from either of you, yet you have forced them to do so. If you have been discussing things with them openly from the beginning, problems now will be easier to handle. Too many parents, however, use the children as intermediaries with which to fight one another.

Often it works like this: The father picks up the kids on Saturday morning. He takes them bowling, to a movie, out to eat, piles them with all sorts of junk food and gifts, returns them to their mother, and disappears for a week or two. Then on Tuesday evening at dinner, Johnny doesn't want to eat his green beans.

"Daddy doesn't make me eat green beans," he says.

The statement is loaded. I advise my women patients to respond calmly with a statement such as, "You are living with me now. And my rule is that you eat the green beans."

Johnny is quite likely to say, "I want to go live with Daddy."

You can respond, "I'm sure you would like to live with Daddy. There's part of me that would like to live with Daddy, too. And that's what Daddy and I are working toward." (If, indeed, you are.)

I don't think my husband really enjoys the role of father. Could this be one reason he wants to leave?

Possibly. Separation will give you a chance to see how much your husband really cares for the children. If he doesn't show signs of missing them on a day-to-day basis, then maybe you and the children are better off without him.

My husband spoils the kids on weekends. How can I get him to stop?

Try to have a calm discussion with your husband, and point out that he can stop living with you as your husband but he can never abdicate his role as their father. Explain that his lax discipline on the weekends is not helpful to them in the long run. Try to agree on some ground rules of basic discipline so that the children are faced with reasonably consistent standards.

If the situation is such that your husband refuses to do his part, the best you can do is show your children, through your own behavior, that you are mature and strong, and growing stronger. You should be doing that anyway.

Once we have separated, should I date?

I recommend that you don't, for a while at least. First of all, you are angry, hostile, and particularly vulnerable. If you are working toward a reconciliation, a relationship of your own will compound everyone's problems and make the outlook grim.

Second, you need some time to try out your independence for size, even if you are sure the marriage is over. You must understand why your marriage broke up. It could be hard to find an unmarried person who is right for you, and the subculture of divorced men and women is made up of too many troubled people. All have failed in their earlier attempts to relate to other human beings. Can you dare to involve yourself with yet another man whose life is a complex tangle of emotional interactions with an ex-wife (and who knows how many others)? Give yourself some time. You need to learn how to separate the perennial losers from the ones who have grown since their first experiences. So often I see a woman, freed from her first marriage, run out and latch onto exactly the same type of man she married the first time around.

Even if you find a true lover, even if you *know* that this time it is different, the children need time to adjust. Another man around the house is a sure sign of their father's "death," and they may respond with unmistakable signs of grief. Sometimes their adverse reactions can contribute to another separation.

My husband is seeing several women. Do I have to stay home and do nothing while he's having the time of his life?

Of course not. You can still have a fulfilling social life. Play sports. Volunteer for charity work or church activities. Take a class or two. Get out and be active. Meet many different kinds of people. Grow. If you do, you will not feel desperate to meet another man right away. You will become more independent and will know yourself and the qualities you are looking for in a man much better.

Sometimes I feel edgy. How long should I wait before having sex with another man?

It is always difficult to answer such a question, because the answer depends upon many factors. How long you can go without a sexual release will depend upon how you have used and viewed sex. Some women who found sex a duty may be relieved. Others who used it as an escape, a pacifier, a sedative, a reassurance for their own failing self-confidence, will naturally find it more difficult to put sex aside for a time.

I believe that you should try to put sex into perspective in your life and not feel that it must be part of a new dating experience. Holding off on sex may not seem fair, but it will probably save you a lot of pain in the long run.

A patient named Andrea was separated and waiting for her divorce from her husband Mark, who was now living openly as a homosexual. Andrea faced a typical dilemma. The single men at work (and some of the married ones) all tried to seduce her. It is popular mythology among men that a formerly married woman is "used merchandise" and ready to hop into bed with anyone who shows her a little attention. In the throes of a near-depression from her disastrous marriage to Mark, Andrea found herself in bed one morning with one of the men from her office. It was the day of her session with me, and she cried through most of the hour.

"If it upsets you so, do you have any idea why you went to bed with him?" I asked.

"I don't know. I really don't know. I don't even like

the guy. But he took me to dinner, and I've been so lonely, and . . . well . . ." She was silent.

"Tell me about him," I suggested. "What's he like?"

"Well, he's very sophisticated. About twenty-four. Never been married. Tall and blonde, kind of lean. He's . . . well, he's always been very nice. He never tried anything with me when Mark and I were together —like a lot of the other guys did. He respected me, I thought."

"He's soft-spoken?" I asked.

"Yes."

"Sharp dresser?"

"Yes."

"He was very considerate of you . . . pulled out your chair, lit your cigarettes, opened doors for you?"

"Yes," Andrea acknowledged, looking at me strangely.

"He invited you back to his apartment to listen to some music—classical, probably. You had a glass of wine?"

"Sherry."

"You weren't really attracted to him physically, even though he's good-looking. What you really liked was the gentle way he treated you, right?" Andrea nodded. She must have been sure I could read her mind.

"Then he leaned over and kissed you. You were surprised, but it made you feel warm inside. You felt reassured that you were still attractive to men. Then very gently, but before you really had time to object, he walked you into the bedroom and made love to you."

There were tears in her eyes as she shook her head.

"It was a great feeling when he was kissing you, but you felt no passion for him during the sex?"

"No. But . . . how did you know all this?"

"From many of the things you told me before. In my opinion, you aren't ready for sex yet with another man."

"What do you mean?"

"Think about what kind of man he is, how gentle he is, how sophisticated, how—"

"How much like Mark," Andrea interrupted. She looked shocked.

"It's not unusual at all," I said. "Because you haven't learned to understand yourself, you chose the same sort of man you picked in the first place. He is not necessarily a homosexual, but he has many of the same character traits as Mark. You seem to be drawn to a gentle, nonthreatening type of man who treats you with a great deal of respect. You find him ultimately unsatisfying in bed. It's too soon, Andrea. You don't really know yet what kind of man is good for you.

"Whatever weaknesses your husband had, you chose him as your lover. Until you understand more about your own personality, you run the danger of making the same mistake twice."

My husband says he wants to come back home. What should I tell him?

You have to decide whether you want him back. Perhaps you can see that your separation has caused him to mature. Perhaps he has been able to recognize some of his own weaknesses and he is trying to repair them. Perhaps he has shown himself to be a loving, caring father in spite of the troubles between you.

On the other hand, you may have realized that his

weaknesses are beyond repair. Perhaps he is still running around with other women and merely wants the convenience of living at home. When you feel emotionally stable and ready to continue life on your own, you must weigh your options carefully. Talk to a lawyer so that you understand your legal rights. Talk to a professional counselor so you understand the emotional considerations. Then you must decide.

Be honest with your feelings. If you submerge them once again, you will only compound the problems. I believe that every marriage that can be saved should be saved. But I am enough of a realist to know that not every marriage can work, even when both partners want it to.

You must be strong enough to face the truth—one way or the other.

How long should I allow a separation to continue?

Separation is an intermediate stage. It is a time when husband and wife can rediscover their love for one another, or it can be the first step toward divorce.

Separation should not be allowed to continue as a permanent situation. Your state laws probably provide for a mandatory period of separation prior to divorce. That will be a guideline for you. As a general rule, I would say that during about six months and two years of living apart, you and your husband should be able to come to a final decision about the fate of your marriage.

CHAPTER
11

Getting Back Together

Can we ever get our marriage back to the way it was?

You must do better than that. The way it was was unhealthy. The way it was resulted in cheating. You must work to make your marriage *better* than it was before. Whether or not you separated from your husband physically, you have been separated emotionally by the act of adultery. When the two of you decide to give your marriage another try, you face a lot of difficult —but potentially rewarding—work.

I can't get the other woman out of my mind. How can I work on improving our marriage?

The first few weeks and months are going to be the

most trying. Remember the guiding principle: *The important thing is not his relationship with the other woman; it is his relationship with you.* With that thought imbedded in your mind, you have to guard against the temptation to ply him with questions about the affair. You have to be careful not to place uncalled-for restrictions upon him. In the past, he may not have accounted for every moment of his time, and making him do so now will only cause him to chafe. Don't insist that he promise to stay away from the other woman. Remember, he is constantly evaluating his marriage against a picture of living with her or in what he may think of as swinging bacherlorhood. If you continue to pressure him because of his adultery, he will be motivated to call it quits.

What *should* I do to help our marriage?

It is far better for you to go on the offensive. If you have studied the preceding chapters carefully, you should have some idea of what went wrong and how you can begin to change.

First, try to talk with your husband about whatever it is that is coming between the two of you. Get the problem out in the open so you both see it clearly. Then start to spend more time together. Take up the same hobby. Travel together. Think of activities you used to enjoy together and try them again. Work as hard at being together as you have been working at staying apart.

A patient named Jim had season tickets to the Philadelphia Eagles football games. Usually he took one of the other men in the office to the game with him. But one blustery Sunday afternoon shortly after he and his wife Ellen had reconciled, he invited Ellen to go with him. She had misgivings about leaving her "baby" at home (he was three years old), but she was trying to follow my advice and spend more time with her husband. She wasn't really a football fan, but she agreed to go.

As they rode to the stadium, Jim began to share some of his thoughts with Ellen. He was concerned that she was being overprotective of their son, and he admitted that it sometimes made him feel neglected. As a result, he took refuge in long hours of work. He admitted some of his own guilt in that respect, for he had encouraged Ellen to smother the child with care.

Ellen finally began to understand their problems more fully. She had used motherhood as an excuse to escape from Jim. He had used work as an escape from her. But why did they need to escape from one another? What were they running away from? And what problems were they creating for their son in the process? For the first time, they seriously discussed their actions.

Ellen didn't know if she could change, but she agreed to try. Jim said he would, too. He would do his part to help his son begin the overdue process of separating from his mother. Both Ellen and Jim had a large task in front of them, but that day was a turning point in their marriage. Now they both knew they were working to strengthen it. The Eagles lost that day, but Ellen and Jim won.

How can we begin to come closer together?

Tennis, ceramics classes, lectures, dining out, community projects, travel—there are thousands of activities that the two of you can enjoy together.

You should also try to share whatever aspects of your lives you have closed off from one another. Perhaps he has kept the family finances secret. You should be an equal partner in the marriage, and as such, you have every right to know how the money is being spent—and perhaps you can relieve your husband of some of the financial worry merely by sharing it. Perhaps you have been excluding him from decisions around the house. He has the right to help choose wallpaper for the hall bathroom.

Amid all this you may discover one other great adventure you are sharing—the reconstruction of your marriage. You may learn that you can talk seriously about the problems in your relationship without berating one another. Maybe you and your husband will become friends once again.

Before we had our problems, my husband and I never really talked with one another about our feelings and our frustrations. How can we begin to talk more freely with one another?

First, you must agree that you *need* to talk more freely. Before being able to do so, you might have to explore why it is that you have been unable to talk. Maybe he had parents who never did, so he had no one to learn from. Or maybe when you tried to communicate as a child you were told to shut up or you were ignored. Or he was considered a sissy to show his feelings, or your siblings laughed at you because you were too sensitive.

Once you have examined these reasons, try to begin to discuss how you feel *now,* not how you felt years ago. If he should refuse, don't press him for his feelings—you still can make an attempt to describe yours. Perhaps when he listens to you for a period of time, he will get used to it and start to talk himself.

What if he doesn't begin to talk to me?

Then this becomes one more reason to consider separation or divorce.

My husband and I are thinking about having a child. Will this bring us closer together?

Not necessarily. When a marriage is already ailing, children might place a strain upon it that will break it up completely. Children are lovable, but they are also a lot of hard work. I would never prescribe pregnancy as a remedy for an ailing marriage.

But if you can see that you are making real progress in overcoming the problems in your relationship, and if you are reasonably optimistic about the future, then you may find that parenthood will fortify your marriage.

Our sex life had deteriorated before my husband cheated. How can we improve it now?

Some couples find sex to be the most difficult aspect of reconciliation. The more insecure the woman, the more difficult it is for her to forgive her husband. The more insecure the man, the more difficult it is for him to overcome his guilt. He may experience a temporary problem with impotence as he struggles with his conscience. It is in bed where the memories of the affair often persist the longest. But try to approach sexual and emotional reconciliation in the same manner. If you have never really talked about sex, you should begin now. This may be difficult for you both, but try. Share feelings with each other that you may have been hiding for years.

Sexual compatibility requires practice. The time it involves is one of the greatest arguments against casual sex. You must talk and feel and experiment with one another in bed to find out what you both like and dislike, what you can both tolerate occasionally, and what are the absolute limits. That can be one of the most pleasurable and uniting experiences in a marriage.

It all sounds good, but my husband and I have both tried to begin discussions of sex, and we just can't seem to talk about it openly. What can we do?

Try this: Sit down one evening and make a list of sexual positions, practices, and techniques. Have your husband make up a list of his own, but don't show your lists to each other just yet. Then label each item with a yes, no, or maybe.

You may discover, to your surprise, that both of you want to be more adventurous in bed. You may both be willing to try a variety of new sexual techniques on one another but are afraid to talk about them. When you compare your lists, you will have a better idea of the boundaries of sexual experimentation that you will each be comfortable with.

You may find the *maybe* column to be the most interesting one of all.

My husband engaged in wild sexual practices with the other woman. Should I try them now?

A word of caution. Don't overdo it. Many wives resolve that they are suddenly going to live up to their husbands' wildest sexual fantasies. A woman decides to give her husband anything and everything he wants in bed. A newfound willingness to experiment is healthy, but it should be genuine. Don't force yourself to do things that, at the moment, you find repulsive, for you may end up resenting your husband even more. It is better to discuss sex with your husband and indicate that you are interested in trying new things together, but that you may have to do so gradually.

My husband and I both want to save our marriage. Yet we have both come to believe that the two of us can never remain completely faithful to one another. Can we maintain a marriage like this?

You are talking about working out an arrangement, as Liz and David did. Yes, arrangements can succeed. But there is one special requirement: *You must both be consciously aware that you are settling for a compromise.* Once both husband and wife accept this fact, their relationship has a better chance of working. The essence of compromise is that each party gets some of what it wants, but not all.

If the arrangement is unconscious (if the husband and wife have not discussed it), then the couple will be unhappy, because both husband and wife will be missing out on something. If it is conscious, then both will understand what they are getting from the relationship and why they have to give up some things. Arrangements that work usually do not get to the psychiatrist's office. Those that do not work often wind up in therapy.

An arrangement is a means to stabilize an unhealthy relationship, and consequently it is a substitute for a normal way of life. And as with all substitutes, you will always feel that something is missing. Are you willing to settle for that?

My husband wants to try "swinging." Will this help our marriage?

Swinging is a type of arrangement whereby each person commits adultery with the consent of, and often in the presence of, the other. Swinging clubs are active throughout the country, and their members often include some of the most prominent and influential people in a city. Some couples claim that swinging seems to help their marriage. The key is the degree of honesty and understanding that the couple have. They must view their swinging as a compromise from the ideal of an exclusive one-man, one-woman relationship. They must understand that they are making tradeoffs, and both partners must freely agree to do so.

Unfortunately, many swinging couples have no idea of what they are really doing. Often the husband or the wife agrees to swinging as a last-ditch chance to save the marriage. Once the reality of the behavior is confronted, the reluctant partner feels worse than ever, and the marriage often collapses. If you are contemplating an arrangement such as this, I recommend that you seek professional counseling first. You and your husband must be totally convinced that it is what you want.

My husband and I are back together. And we are happy. But sometimes I wake up in the middle of the night crying. The memory of his affair stays with me. Will I ever be able to forget what happened?

No. But although the memory will remain with you always, your feelings about it should change. Pain has a way of being dulled by time and understanding. If you do your emotional homework, you will find the resentment and bitterness dying. You will realize that you and your husband shared the responsibility for the affair. You will understand the psychological reasons that caused your husband to turn to someone else and caused you to react the way you did. You cannot forget, but you can forgive.

What are the chances that my husband will cheat once again?

When you recover from an illness, you may be susceptible to a relapse. If you follow your doctor's advice to eat the proper food and get adequate exercise and sleep, you will be stronger and better prepared to fight off a relapse. Nevertheless, you can contract the same illness again.

The same is true of emotional illness. The emotional weaknesses that contributed to the adultery can never be fully eradicated. A person can shore up his or her defenses but can never be fully out of danger. (Even if you have undergone a relatively successful course of psychotherapy to help you understand the source of your behavior—even if you know your marriage is stronger—there are no guarantees of total health in the future.) What you have learned about yourself and your marriage in dealing with infidelity should make you better prepared to handle stress. If both you and your husband have developed an ability to understand one another, if you are becoming better able to withstand psychological pain, if you are nurturing a capacity to change, if you are developing patience–and if you are both willing to try to work together–the chances of your husband's cheating in the future will be lessened.

I can't wait until I'm able to relax again. But can I ever be sure my husband won't cheat?

No. You can never sit back and assume that everything will be okay. Like an exotic house plant, a marriage must be properly fed and nurtured, given adequate sunlight, and treated with tender loving care. A marriage never ever achieves a state of equilibrium. It either continues to grow because of your efforts, or it withers and dies.

My husband and I spend most of our free time watching television together. Why don't I feel as though I'm sharing anything with him?

I'm amazed that so many couples have the mistaken belief that the normal evening activity for an American family is to stare in silence at the television set. Not only does the tube prevent couples from strengthening their relationship, it also, thanks to the jaded values of the industry, gives them a totally distorted view of reality. They see husbands and wives in conflicts that are usually portrayed superficially and resolved unrealistically. And their children get a view of a society so troubled that it can only solve its problems with violence.

If you must watch television, you can make it a more

positive experience. Watch only a few shows and then turn the television off to discuss the thoughts and opinions elicited by what you just saw. Try to understand the motivation behind the behavior of the characters. Talk about what annoyed you about the show and what you liked about it. But talk. Come together mentally and emotionally. Don't let the television get between you and your loved ones.

Will there be certain times and occasions when my husband may be more susceptible to a relapse?

Yes. One common occurrence is an "anniversary" reaction, which we mentioned in Chapter 1. A woman developed emotional problems as the result of an incident at a New Year's Eve party. The approach of another holiday season gave rise to a relapse of her emotional problems. The same can happen to you and your husband. If he had a brief affair on a business trip to Chicago, he might find himself uneasy when he has to return to the same city. You might be irritable and more suspicious when he returns.

You can never be totally safe from anniversary reactions, but if you are aware of them, you can sometimes handle them more easily. If your husband must return to Chicago, share your anxieties with him. Let him know that you understand the basis for your suspicion. Talk about it together. He may in turn share with you his own uncertain feelings about returning to the scene of his "crime."

What can we do to guard against a relapse of cheating?

While there are no guarantees, there are steps you

can take to prevent another instance of infidelity. Each experience in life changes us. You are not the same person you were twenty years ago, last year, last month, or yesterday. One hopes that you and your husband have undergone positive personality changes that have made your relationship stronger. What is marriage all about, anyway? What do you want out of it? How can you change your relationship for the better? (Where do you want it to go?)

At this stage in therapy, I often ask husband and wife to make separate lists of what they believe to be the good aspects of their marriage and what qualities they each want in a spouse. Surprisingly, many people don't know what they want. And if they don't know, how can their spouses please them? Husbands and wives need to spend long hours in discussion, learning, perhaps for the first time, what the other expects out of marriage and how each can provide for the other's needs. Honesty, even if it is painful, is crucial at this time.

CHAPTER
12

Prevention

Are there danger signals to watch for that might indicate we are heading for trouble before any cheating occurs?

Yes. A person can cheat without having sex. You need to be aware of how much of what I call noncheating cheating may be going on in your marriage.

Noncheating cheating is important to recognize because it frequently precedes physical adultery. If you can learn to recognize these patterns, you may be able to prevent any further adultery from disrupting your marriage.

What is noncheating cheating?

It is simply anything that you or your husband allow

to become an emotional lover. You let it come between you, and it sets up an emotional barrier.

What is the most common form of noncheating cheating?

It is probably "workaholism." Not only is this a very common form of noncheating cheating, but it may be the most difficult to defend against. How can a doctor's wife get mad at her husband for working so hard to save lives? How can your husband berate you for working overtime at your job in order to pay the extra family bills? We are conditioned by society to believe that work is good. Many of us—especially men—measure our self-worth by the amount of work we accomplish.

Two of my patients, Mary and Glen, are classic workaholics. Glen is twenty-nine, the youngest CPA in a firm of tax accountants. He has a legitimate reason for working extra hours to get himself established in the practice. Mary, now twenty-seven, takes care of her two small children and also attends night school in order to complete her degree so that she, too, can advance in her career as a design engineer. But they paid a price for this dedication to duty. They grew apart from one another. Glen had an affair.

This is a common predicament for young professional couples. Hard work is necessary to get ahead in life—but how much is enough? In the beginning of my psychiatric practice, I had a tendency to overwork, feeling that I needed to see every person who needed help. It didn't take long for me to realize that even if I opened my office twenty-four hours a day, I would not be able to solve everyone's problems.

But we have to work hard just to make ends meet, don't we?

Sure you do, but you must keep it in perspective. You have to be an emotionally healthy person if you are going to work up to your potential. Giving of yourself to your family—and receiving love and support in return—will make you a more fulfilled human being. Even if you don't have a paying job, you know there is always more housework to be done. Some people feel guilty whenever they aren't working.

By interrelating with the members of your family, you gain experience and empathy, and thus you are able to do your job better, whatever that job is. President Carter seems to be in touch with this belief. He has advised his staff workers to spend more time with their families.

How can I stop being a workaholic?

Perhaps the way to balance career considerations with family ones is to think in terms of quality of time rather than quantity of time. Make the most of the opportunities you have to be with your family. If you or your husband feel that you must work overly hard during the week, try to set aside a segment of the weekend that will be just for the family. Let nothing but a genuine emergency interfere with that plan.

No matter how busy you and your husband are, you cannot afford to let your lives move ahead separately. Never again will you be able to share the joys of helping your children grow. When your six-year-old is sixteen, she will no longer want to sit on your lap and hear a story. No business deal, no matter how big, can bring the same look of unabashed glory that crosses the face of a twelve-year-old when he knows his parents saw him slide safely into home plate.

Sure, take care of business. But take care of home, too.

What are other forms of noncheating cheating?

Parents and other relatives often become a barrier between husband and wife. Any marriage that includes a third adult is going to run into some degree of trouble sooner or later. The case history in Chapter 7 is a classic example.

But my parents are getting old. Don't I have a responsibility to care for them as they age?

Older couples often submit to this duty. There are occasional situations when a certain amount of care is definitely your responsibility. But you must never let your aging parents come between you and your husband.

For fifteen long years, Louise, one of my patients, has been trying to cope with her mother-in-law's living with her and her husband. Henry's mother, who is now seventy-seven, still thinks of him as her baby. Consequently, she wants to cook all the meals, iron his clothes, and perform all the duties that Louise did during the early years of her marriage. Louise is quite naturally upset, jealous, and hurt. Her mother-in-law is a constant source of tension. What's more, Louise and Henry find it difficult to make love in a relaxed manner, knowing that Mother is sleeping in the next room.

But won't I feel guilty if I neglect Mother?

The decision to take over at least some of the responsibility of caring for Mother or Father must be made with extreme care. Does Mother really have to live in the same house? Could she move to an apartment a couple of blocks away? Is she so sick that she will require the care of a nursing home? You must search your soul for the answers to these questions. Of course, you don't want to mistreat your parents, but can you risk your marriage to pay back an old "debt"?

My husband complains that I spend so much time with the children that he never gets to see me. Could I be using them as a form of noncheating cheating?

Unfortunately, yes. Some people marry just to have children.

A woman named Carrie did this, and once her son was born, she immediately began to use him as an excuse to stay away from her husband. She smothered the child with care, doing everything for him and attempting to guard him against potential bruises. She carried the boy constantly and took him with her wherever she went.

By the time Louise's son was three years old, he was still not walking properly. Her husband developed a genuine feeling of jealousy. In an emotional sense, his young son had become his wife's lover. Part of his motivation in having an affair was the need to strike back.

Children are the future. They are the new generation of people who will carry on with the business of life. Yet they must not be used to insulate you from the realities of an unhappy marriage. If you pamper your children as a means of escaping from your husband, you do double harm: Not only do you jeopardize your marriage, but you risk raising those children with their own twisted values.

My husband spends all his free time with his best friend. They are together constantly. Could he be using this as a form of noncheating cheating?

Yes. We all need friends, because no one person—even a spouse—can fulfill our every need. But friendship can be overdone. It should never come ahead of marriage.

How do I know if I'm spending too much time with my girl friend?

Do you spend hours each day on the telephone together? Do you believe you have to check with her before you make even small decisions? Do you feel that you must have as many new clothes as she? Are you upset if you have a bowling date with her and can't keep it because one of the children is sick?

These are all danger signals that you may be spending too much time and emotional effort trying to please your friend instead of your family. It is a sign that you may really still be an emotional adolescent, more concerned about the opinions of your peers than your family.

My husband has a friend at work, a bachelor, who has started to come home with him almost every day. He

sits around during the evening and watches television with us, or we play cards. Are we using him as a barrier?

There is a subculture of single adults who sort of adopt a married couple. Every night finds them together. Soon the single person expects their company and feels hurt when he or she is not invited along on every outing. There may or may not be sexual overtones to this sort of relationship, but a married couple usually allow this to happen only because they are not yet ready and able to settle into their own one-to-one relationship.

My husband spends all his spare time working on cars. Is it right for me to feel jealous?

Cars, boats, CB radios, and other such things often come between a couple. A complaint I often hear is, "He takes care of the car better than he takes care of me." Golf widows and fishing widows are also subject to noncheating cheating husbands. Women, too, tend to cheat by concentrating on their own hobbies, such as macrame, charity work, and tennis.

Hobbies are an important part of life. They help us round out our interests and abilities. It is good for a husband and wife to share a hobby, and it is also healthy for them to spend some time on a hobby separately. But whenever the hobby begins to interfere with what should be normal interaction between husband and wife, it has become dangerous to your marriage.

How can I tell when a hobby gets out of hand?

Perhaps the signal to look for is when one of you expresses a desire to sit down and have a serious discussion and the other says, "I can't talk now, because I have to wax the car . . ." or whatever.

Before my husband really did have an affair, he used to say that the racetrack was his mistress. Was he really joking?

Gambling is a hobby that can cause a rift between husband and wife. The key to all forms of noncheating cheating is excess. A night at the races once in a while may cost no more than a weekly golf game. An occasional late poker game can be a good way to blow off steam. But an obsessive-compusive gambler who is losing great amounts of money (and depriving his family while doing so) is probably ill. In addition to other emotional problems caused by his gambling, he is also cheating on you.

I feel that my husband drinks too much. In the first place, he spends too much time around bars. Also, I feel that drinking lowers his moral standards. He met his girl friend in a bar. What should I do?

If you are married to an alcoholic, you may be doomed to spending countless evenings watching him snore in front of the television or waiting for him to drag himself home in the wee hours of the morning (if he comes home at all). Family dinners will be ruined, holidays spoiled, vacations avoided. The children may witness violent arguments and physical abuse. They may well suffer from nightmares. An alcoholic husband may be impotent; an alcoholic wife may be frigid. Alcoholism can ruin your marriage just as surely as adultery—and frequently the two go together.

Alcoholism is a disease that needs treatment—the earlier the better.

I have been drinking heavily since I found out about my husband's affair. How can I tell if I am drinking too much?

Ask yourself the following questions:

- When you get up in the morning, do you worry about how much you had to drink the night before?
- Are you angry with yourself for drinking last night, even if you only had "a couple"?
- Do you find yourself looking at the clock, wishing it were time for that first drink at the end of the workday?
- Do you need to drink to get through the evening at home with your husband?
- Do you drink because you feel it will help you respond better in bed?

If the answer to many of these questions is yes, there may be a problem beginning in your marriage that you had better think about. Since you are faced with a crisis because your husband has cheated on you, now is not the time to burden yourself with a drinking problem.

Can drugs be used in the same manner as alcohol?

Definitely. The use of hard drugs such as heroin, morphine, cocaine, and amphetamines is clearly going to damage your marriage as well as your health. Softer drugs like marijuana and hashish may or may not have a place in your life. If they do, you must understand that they are just as capable of being abused as is liquor. There are those who smoke pot much the same way as others have an occasional cocktail before dinner. But some people remain stoned, just as their alcoholic friends remain bombed.

A patient named Janet had been so upset by her husband's affair that she had difficulty sleeping and, in turn, getting ready for work in the morning. I decided to give her a prescription for a sedative so she could sleep. During our session the following week, she seemed vague and listless. When I asked about her condition, she admitted she had taken a pill that morning. I reminded her that I had given them to her only to help her sleep. I didn't want her to use them during the day.

Janet promised she would be careful, but the following week she was even more unresponsive. And she tried to withhold the truth about her medication. Finally she admitted that she had been taking the pills every day–sometimes in double and triple doses. She had obtained another prescription from her family doctor.

"Janet, I know you are going through a difficult time," I said. "I understand that you are suffering, but *you* must understand what the pills are doing to you. You and Gary have problems–serious problems. The pills can help you forget about them for a time. But when the pills wear off, the problems will still be there. You need to work with Gary to help solve them, and you can't do that when you are half-asleep."

Janet promised to stay off the medicine. But from time to time over the next year, she escaped into that dream world. Her marriage ultimately broke up. I don't know if it could have been saved, but she really didn't give it a chance.

This is the most insidious aspect of drug abuse. It prevents you from dealing with reality.

Are there any more kinds of noncheating cheating?

There is another type that we should discuss. It is sometimes used by couples who have no children or whose children are grown. Let me illustrate.

A man came to me one day with a problem. He had married his second wife when he was fifty and she was thirty-five. Neither of them wanted children at this stage of life. Shortly after they were married, they adopted a stray kitten. They fed it, fixed up a bed and litter box in one corner of their small house, and took it to the vet for treatment. In my office, the man complained that his wife soon began to pay more attention to the cat than to him. She held the animal over her shoulder, patted its back, and talked baby talk to it. She spent hours in the evening playing with it. She bought it birthday presents and Christmas presents. Then she began to nag her husband to buy a bigger house, so that the cat would have its own room. She threatened to leave him if he didn't. After dipping into his retirement savings to buy a new house, his wife moved *his* bed into the spare room. She slept with the *cat!*

Try as we might, we could not persuade her to come in for therapy. Unable to tolerate this noncheating cheating any longer, the man sued for divorce.

This is an extreme case. But be careful that your

cuddly pet doesn't interfere with your opportunities to cuddle your husband.

If my husband does have an affair again, how will I be able to cope with it? Won't it be even worse for me?

Initially, you will probably suffer the same feelings of pain, anguish, and rejection. Perhaps they will not be as severe as the first time, for you have learned not to expect perfection in human beings. And perhaps the next time you will be better prepared to evaluate the situation objectively. If the relapse is a single incident occurring in a moment of weakness, you may decide to continue working to strengthen your marriage. But if your husband failed to learn any lessons from his previous mistake—or even if he does have a better understanding of his behavior but still persists in adultery—you must bravely face the likelihood of divorce. He may be "terminally ill" emotionally—unable to change. If so, you have to look out for your own interests.

CHAPTER 13

Divorce

How do I know if and when my marriage is finished?

When a marriage is dead, it should be buried. But very few people seem to know when the heart has stopped beating.

The final decision is rarely made quickly, nor should it be. Usually a separation occurs first, and even the most bitter of spouses often wavers between reconciliation and divorce. No one wants to feel like a failure. In most states, the legal process of getting a divorce takes a year or more, and I think this waiting period is good. It provides an opportunity to make up your mind for sure—if you put the time to good use.

Frequently one or both persons really wants a divorce but cannot bring the decision out into the open. This results in a series of separations and reconciliations, fights and peace treaties, good times and bad. The critical symptom in such a relationship is *lack of change.* Separations and fights are painful, but they can also be beneficial to a marriage if they cause the partners to do basic work on their personalities and relationship. However, when a couple undergo this trauma again and again without really changing themselves or the situation, they may have irreconcilable differences.

This was the case with a patient of mine named Martha. Her husband Bob, whom she'd married right after graduating from high school, was a womanizer—a lifelong cheater. He had come in for a few sessions at Martha's request, and I soon could tell that he had very deep-rooted inabilities to relate normally to other human beings. Because of her own therapy, Martha had come to see that Bob probably would never change his behavior. Though he might promise to remain faithful, before long, he would be out chasing after other women again.

Even so, a part of Martha still loved Bob. No one slips out of a long-standing marriage without feelings of guilt and failure. Martha wanted to believe Bob's promises that he would change, even though she had heard them many times before. I asked them to come in for a joint session to discuss their future. It is the counselor's job to try to measure the degree of change that is taking place during the course of separation—change for the better or the worse. I do not try to make the decisions for my patients, but I try to make sure they understand each other's position. Frequently they seem to have difficulty hearing what the other is saying.

During one of our meetings, when Bob was on his best behavior, he looked at Martha tenderly and said, "I'd really like to move back home and—"

"And do what you've always done," Martha interrupted.

"No, honey, no. It's going to be different this time. I promise I'll—"

"I want to believe you, Bob, but I'm tired of your promises. I've heard them so many times before."

"You've referred to the past again, Martha." I pointed out. "You seem to be having a great deal of difficulty coping with what has happened—so much so that you find it difficult to talk about the future with Bob. I wonder . . . do you really want him back?"

Now the years of anguish and indecision reached their climax. Martha could see that her own longing to have this unfaithful husband back was a reflection of some unhealthy needs of her own. She summoned up her courage, took a deep breath, and said, "I want a divorce."

In separate sessions, we discussed the pros and cons of splitting up. Martha was lonely and depressed. But there were things she liked about living without a husband for the first time in her adult life.

I asked her the crucial question: Did she notice any real changes in Bob over the months of their separation? She shook her head no. The more we talked, the more she became sure of her decision. Occasionally over the next few months, she would waver, especially when Bob would call and try to convince her to change her mind. But those periods became less frequent as she grew happier living without him. Bob stopped seeing me when he realized that therapy would not bring about a reconciliation. As Martha suspected, he soon continued his endless quest to prove his manhood.

Look over what has happened to your marriage since you learned of your husband's affair. Here is a checklist of questions to ask yourself to determine whether things have been changing for the better:

- Have you begun to communicate more fully with one another?
- Do you spend more quality time together?
- Have you both been willing to agree upon what you expect from each other in terms of your relationship, sex, and the day-to-day responsibilities of raising a family?
- Are you more comfortable being together now?
- Do you look forward to seeing one another?
- Have you made your marriage a priority?
- Has your sex life improved?
- Have you been able to stop holding the affair over your husband's head?
- If you showed symptoms of anxiety, depression, alcoholism, or drug abuse, have those symptoms diminished?
- Are you less angry?
- Are you still willing to work to save your marriage? Is your husband?

If you answer yes to at least half of these questions, you are well on your way to a reconciliation. If not, you must now consider the definite possibility of divorce.

My husband wants to move back home, but I think I want a divorce. What is the best way to tell him?

Telling him in person is best, for it will probably make you feel better in the long run. Gently but firmly say, "I want a divorce." Have your reasons in mind, so that you can explain them. There is a good chance that he knows them all and will simply have to acknowledge the strength of your reasoning.

If you can't summon the courage to tell him to his face, you can always let him know your decision over the phone, in a letter, or by having an attorney prepare and serve divorce papers.

The thought of divorce makes me feel like such a failure. How can I overcome this?

You will feel better if you keep in perspective the *degree* of guilt you bear. Sure the marriage was a failure. But everybody makes mistakes. You did play some part in the death of the marriage, as did your ex-husband. But not all the fault is yours. During the months of anguish following the divorce, try to remember that something positive can come out of every experience.

I miss my ex-husband. Can I see him after we divorce?

I would advise against spending time with him. Many divorced women experience a feeling of total loss, since, as I have explained, they have been conditioned to measure their self-worth by their ability to please a man. That way of thinking should be in the past. When you decided to divorce, you decided to face life on your own—at least for a while.

You cannot continue to visit the grave of your marriage. As with any death, you are going to experience a certain amount of shock. Cry out your grief. Let the tears wash away some of the pain. Then get up, dry your eyes, and get busy with your new duties.

Can I go out to dinner with him every so often?

This is not a good idea. If you find that you really must discuss something with him, such as the kids or the equity in the house, you do not need to go out to dinner. That tends to be too romantic at a time when you are lonely and vulnerable. Keep the moments of personal contact short and reserved. Guard against getting into the same old fights or—and this is fairly common—hopping back into the same old bed. If you chose to divorce, you did so because you perceived problems that could not be solved. To reestablish contact with your ex-husband is to open the door to those problems once more. Forget him. The marriage is finished.

What happens if the car breaks down?

As far as possible, you must stop depending upon your husband. If the car is due for inspection, take it to be inspected. If the drain pipe is clogged, unclog it or call a plumber. If mail arrives for your ex-husband, forward it. If a telephone call comes, give the caller his new number. There should be very few reasons to contact him. Learn to solve your own problems, and keep the contact with your ex-husband at a minimum.

My husband has a good job. We had a comfortable life together. How can I now adjust to a lower standard of living?

The less you depend upon your ex-husband for financial support, the happier you will be. If there is less money to go around, so be it.

Dorothy was typical. She spent fifteen years employed as a housewife. Now divorced, she still depended totally on her ex-husband to make the monthly child-support and alimony payments. When he threatened to cut off the money supply, Dorothy sobbed her worries out to me in the office. When she had calmed down, I asked simply, "Why don't you get a job?"

"What could I do? I haven't worked in years."

"Have you looked for a job?"

"No."

"Well, how long do you think you will be dependent upon the money from Fred?"

"I don't know. I hadn't really thought about it."

"A year?"

"I don't know."

"Two years? Five? Ten? What about when the children are all grown up and living on their own? Fred won't be paying child support, and he certainly won't want to pay alimony."

"I guess I'll work then. But maybe I'll be married again."

"Dorothy, you have to start looking at the positive side of this divorce. It is giving you the chance to make it on your own. I know it would be nice to have a loving husband. And it would be a bonus if he earned a good salary. But you don't have that. Even if you do remarry, it may not be for a few years. Why don't you take this chance to go out into the world and prove to yourself that you can survive?"

Dorothy promised to try. She found a neighbor who agreed to watch the children after school. Then she started answering want ads in the paper. After several interviews, she landed a job as a nurse's aide. Before long, with the help of a vocational rehabilitation agency, she entered training to become a licensed practical nurse. Her paycheck is not nearly as big as the one Fred used to bring home, but she has learned to live on it. She learned, also, that she is not a helpless child. She is a capable adult.

I'm so afraid of the future. What can I expect in the next few months and years?

The period following the decision to divorce will bring a variety of uncomfortable feelings and situations. You may feel like a misfit among your married friends, and, indeed, you may find that they are no longer your friends. Your children may avoid you because they feel frustrated at not being able to make you happy. If you hold a job merely for financial reasons, your work may leave you unfulfilled. Men may automatically assume that you are sexually active, and they will keep up constant pressure for you to "give in." There will be lonely nights with nowhere to go and no one to talk to. You will think about what went wrong and feel guilty about what you think you should have done to save the marriage. You will have a dismal future—if you allow it to remain dismal.

Or you can begin to take an active role in solving your problems. Find out what other divorced women are doing and how they made it past their early periods of depression. Change your circle of friends. Join organizations that will put you in contact with men who share some of your interests. Keep busy accomplishing something.

Some women find divorce to be one of the most stimulating experiences of their lives, once the initial pain and anger have passed. After years of depending upon a man to supply their needs and desires, they learn to enjoy doing so for themselves. This is the time to forget about what your ex-husband is up to and go out and do your own thing. Work, socialize, and experience life on your own.

I want my children to lead as normal a life as possible. How should I treat them after the divorce?

You cannot shield your children against all the pain, but you can follow some commonsense guidelines that will help them adjust to the new situation as easily as possible. Here is a list of dos and don'ts.

• *Do not berate a child for his or her reaction to Daddy's absence.* The child is grieving for the dead marriage, just as you are. But children often show this sorrow in an indirect manner. Your children may become more mischievous or rebellious. Their schoolwork may be done poorly. They may become fearful and withdrawn. You must try to understand that these are symptoms of their grief. Try to encourage them to speak up about the divorce and how they feel about it. Once their feelings are in the open, you—and they—may be able to deal with them more directly.

• *Do not remove all traces of Daddy.* You have divorced him, but the children have not. Every child needs a true image of both parents so that her or his personality development will not be affected any more than it has already been.

• *Do not "bad-mouth" Daddy.* An understanding of how you both contributed to the breakdown of the marriage will help you keep your feelings in perspective. Do not try to show the children that you are innocent and their father is guilty. Try to speak of him objectively. Let the children decide for themselves, over a period of time, what traits they like about Daddy and what traits they dislike.

• *Do not use a child as a spy.* There is a temptation to grill your children after custodial visits in order to discuss what is happening in your ex-husband's life. Sometimes a divorced wife wants to know all the details about Daddy's latest girl friend, and the child, knowing this, goes out of his or her way to find out. Other times the child is used as sort of courier to pass information back and forth between the parents. You must guard against this. The children should be allowed to maintain their individual relationships with both of you. They should never become caught up in the raging battle of personalities.

• *Let teenage children decide where they want to live.* The other household may not be as bad as you think. A teenage child is old enough to try both parents. A boy, in particular, might wish to try living with his father. If he likes it, he will stay. If he doesn't like it, he has the option of returning to you. But forbidding him to live with his father will only increase his desire to do so. (Of course, where incest has occurred, you would have to consider the child's desire more carefully and probably will need counseling at this point.)

• *Do not force children to go on custodial visits.* An adolescent child, especially, often has things to do on the weekend that are more important to him than a visit with his father. In fact, parental rebellion can be a healthy sign at this stage of life. If a younger child refuses to go, you must talk with him or her to try to find out why. If your child, or the father, has a reason for not spending a certain weekend together, try to be flexible. Adjust your own schedule, as all parents must do from time to time. You must not let the child feel you are trying to get rid of him or her.

• *Spend some time alone with the children.* Some children of divorced parents always find themselves surrounded by their parents' friends, their step-parents, their half-brothers and -sisters, or various aunts and uncles. Every child needs a little time alone with his or her parents. Make sure you supply that time, particularly if you are the noncustodial parent.

• *Do not become jealous if the children become attached to the other woman.*

Your role as a mother is secure. No one can ever replace you in the eyes of your children. If they do show an attachment to the other woman, it is quite likely that they are doing so to please Daddy. They are afraid of losing his love.

• *Do not take children along on dates.* Your children will be very confused about you and Daddy. If you introduce them to a number of other men, their confusion may be heightened. In particular, you should not have sex with men while the children are in the house. Only when you are reasonably sure that you have found a man you will marry (and that should not be soon) should you introduce him into your children's lives for extended periods of time.

• *Keep the children out of the money hassles.* It is fair for your ex-husband to make child-support payments. But it is cruel to use the children as financial go-betweens who ask Daddy for money for extras. If you feel that the children truly do need more money, discuss it with your ex-husband, or, if necessary, work through the court system.

• *Do not "marry" your children.* If you have never established your own identity, you may be vulnerable to placing a child in the role of head of the household. Never tell your son he is the man of the family now. *You* are the head of the family. The children may be expected to help around the house—perhaps a bit more than in the past—but the major responsibility is yours.

How can I raise my children so that they won't have the same problems if and when they marry?

As you have learned from the case histories throughout this book, the reasons for cheating are sometimes far removed from sex. We all have emotional insecurities that make us susceptible to the pressures of life. I believe that the basic personality develops during the first five years of life. After that, of course, all our life experiences continue to strengthen or weaken our inner selves. If you have children, even if you can casually accept your husband's cheating, you owe it to them to uncover the emotional reasons behind your husband's behavior and your own reactions.

There is a Biblical passage (Numbers 14:18) that speaks of "visiting the iniquity of the fathers upon the children unto the third and fourth generation." Emotional weaknesses are like that. They are passed from parent to child, generation after generation. Until you have made an effort to identify and correct those weaknesses (both yours and his) that contributed to your husband's cheating, you run the risk of passing them on to your children.

On the other hand, if your children can see that you have learned from your mistakes, that you have tried to resolve your problems to the best of your ability, they will grow up learning to imitate your strength of purpose. Your careful handling of this painful episode in your life can lessen the chances that your children will have to face the same pain in their own futures.

A Final Word

You are going through what is probably the most difficult time of your life. You may see no answer that does not involve misery and damage. But the same desire for a solution that made you read this book through to the end should sustain you until answers begin to appear. A saying I find comforting is this: God never closes a door unless he opens a window. Keep looking for that window into the new life that awaits you. For out of all this sadness and pain can come growth and knowledge and the foundation for a new life and new happiness.

APPENDIX:

A Crisis Guide

Once you have studied the points raised in this book, you may need to review them quickly in the event that you are facing an immediate problem in your marriage. The following outline is a guide for such moments of crisis:

I. THE SUSPICION STAGE

A. If it is the first time:

1. *Could you be wrong?* Do you have a tendency to overreact? Are you basically a suspicious person? If the answer to any of these questions is yes:
   - Give your husband the benefit of the doubt.
   - Try to search inside yourself to discover why you have a tendency to be overly suspicious.
   - Do not accuse him.

- Do not tell the children or anyone else of your suspicions.

2. *What is the evidence?* Has there been a change in your husband's personality (depression, irritability, irresponsibility, insomnia, excessive drinking, smoking, eating, etc.)? If the answer is yes:
   - Consider the possibility of job pressures, health problems, or other environmental factors.
   - Try to take stock of your marriage. Look for the warning signs of noncheating cheating.
   - Consider whether it is you that has changed rather than he.
   - Be willing to share some of the responsibility for the change in him.
   - Begin to discuss the personality changes with him.
   - Do not yet confront him with your suspicion.
   - Do not yet tell the children.
3. *Is there direct evidence of his cheating* (such as condoms, lipstick stains, mysterious phone calls, etc.)? If the answer is yes:
   - Confront him with the evidence.
   - Try to believe a reasonable explanation.
   - Give him another chance.
4. *If he denies cheating—even in the face of direct evidence—and his explanation isn't reasonable:*
   - Try to give him one more chance even if he has been cheating. Now that he knows he can't get away with it, he may stop.
   - If the evidence disappears, consider the affair to be over. Begin to work at strengthening your marriage in order to prevent a relapse.
   - Do not become obsessed with having to know the truth.

5. *If the symptoms and evidence continue:*
   - Seek counseling from a doctor, lawyer, professional marriage counselor, or clergyman.
6. *If the evidence continues to appear, and he continues to deny cheating:*
   - Begin to consider taking independent action.
   - See a lawyer to determine your rights.
   - Let your husband know your intentions, whatever they are.

B. If it has happened before:

1. Confront your husband as soon as possible with your suspicion.
2. Consider professional counseling more seriously than you did the first time.
3. Talk to the children. Let them know you are having a problem but that you and their father are trying to work it out. Prepare them for the possibility that you will not be successful. But do not tell them that another person is involved unless the evidence is blatant.

II. THE DISCOVERY STAGE

A. If it is the first time:

1. *And your husband admits to cheating:*
   - View the affair as a symptom of something wrong between the two of you.
   - Discuss with him the problems in your marriage, taking into consideration the pressures of life that may have contributed to the affair.
   - Remember to concentrate on your relationship with him, not on his relationship with the other woman.
   - Be willing to share the responsibility for what happened.

- Consider professional counseling if your combined efforts are not enough to resolve the situation.
- Discuss with the children the fact that the two of you are having a rough time but hope to work out your problems. Do not tell them of the affair if it happened discreetly and only once.
- Do not write off the marriage.
- Do not try to contact the other woman.
- Do not tell your friends and relatives.

2. *If he continues to deny cheating:*
   - Proceed as in I-A-4.

B. If it has happened before:

1. *And your husband denies it:*

   a. If it happened only *once* before:
   - Get professional advice.
   - See a lawyer.
   - Consider the use of a private detective to prove to your husband that you mean business.
   - Let the children know that another person is involved.
   - Prepare yourself seriously for living without him.

   b. If he has been cheating frequently but seems sincere in his desire to change:
   - Insist on him getting professional help.
   - Offer to go along to aid in whatever way you can.

   c. If he has been cheating frequently, pays no attention to your feelings, and expects to continue in the same pattern:
   - Ask yourself why you are putting up with it. Are you a masochist? Are you so weak that you cannot face life without him? If so, you need professional help.

- Seriously consider the alternatives of separation, divorce, and arrangement.
- Consider the effects upon the children—not just the effects of separation or divorce, but the effects of continuing to live within a home that is filled with bitterness and hurt.
- Tell your husband of your plans, giving him one final chance to change.
- Let your children know what alternatives you are considering.
- If he wants to go live with the other person, let him.
- Do not take him back unless he has shown evidence of really trying to change.
- Do not take him back more than once.